The Active Soul

About the Cover image of John Brown.

"They did not hang him at once, but reserved him to preach to them. And then there was another great blunder. They did not hang his four followers with him; that scene was still postponed; and so his victory was prolonged and completed. No theatrical manager could have arranged things so wisely to give effect to his behavior and words. And who, think you, was the manager? Who placed the slave-woman and her child, whom he stooped to kiss for a symbol, between his prison and the gallows?"
—Henry David Thoreau,
"The Last Days of John Brown"

MERCER UNIVERSITY PRESS

Endowed by

TOM WATSON BROWN
and
THE WATSON-BROWN FOUNDATION, INC.

The Active Soul

Emerson and *Thoreau* on Reform and Civil Disobedience

Introduced and edited by

William Homestead

MERCER UNIVERSITY PRESS
Macon, Georgia

MUP/ P713

© 2025 by Mercer University Press
Published by Mercer University Press
1501 Mercer University Drive
Macon, Georgia 31207
All rights reserved. This book may not be reproduced in whole or in part, including illustrations, in any form (beyond that copying permitted by Sections 107 and 108 of the U.S. Copyright Law and except by reviewers for the public press), without written permission from the publisher.

29 28 27 26 25   5 4 3 2 1

Books published by Mercer University Press are printed on acid-free paper that meets the requirements of the American National Standard for Information Sciences—Permanence of Paper for Printed Library Materials.

Printed and bound in the United States.

This book is set in Adobe Caslon Pro.

Cover/jacket design by Burt&Burt.

Cover art: "The Last Moments of John Brown," by Thomas Hovenden, The Metropolitan Museum of Art

Library of Congress Cataloging-in-Publication Data
Names: Emerson, Ralph Waldo, 1803-1882, author. | Thoreau, Henry David, 1817-1862, author. | Homestead, William, author.
Title: The active soul : Emerson and Thoreau on reform and civil disobedience / introduced and edited by William Homestead.
Description: Macon, Georgia : Mercer University Press, 2025.
Identifiers: LCCN 2024054729 (print) | LCCN 2024054730 (ebook) | ISBN 9780881468984 (trade paperback) | ISBN 9780881469714 (ebook)
Subjects: LCSH: Antislavery movements. | Slavery. | Civil disobedience. | Justice. | LCGFT: Essays. | Speeches.
Classification: LCC PS1602 .H65 2025 (print) | LCC PS1602 (ebook) | DDC 814/.3--dc23/eng/20241220
LC record available at https://lccn.loc.gov/2024054729
LC ebook record available at https://lccn.loc.gov/2024054730

"The one thing in the world, of value, is the active soul."

Ralph Waldo Emerson, "The American Scholar"

CONTENTS

Introduction: From Abolitionism to Climate Justice   ix

Emerson, The Over-Soul (1841)   1

Thoreau, Civil Disobedience (1849)   27

Emerson, The Fugitive Slave Law (1854)   61

Thoreau, Slavery in Massachusetts (1854)   87

Emerson, John Brown (1860)   111

Thoreau, The Last Days of John Brown (1860)   121

Works Cited   137

INTRODUCTION

FROM ABOLITIONISM TO CLIMATE JUSTICE

Ralph Waldo Emerson and Henry David Thoreau witnessed the beginnings of the Anthropocene: the age of dependent-on-a-healthy-ecosystem humans increasingly putting the screws to the planet. As such, they witnessed the beginnings of endless eco-social crises, all currently exacerbated by climate crisis. Temperatures are rising to a destructive 1.5 degrees Celsius above pre-industrial levels and are heading towards an even more destructive 2.0 or higher, leading to the possible collapse of civilization (as we know it).

Regenerative solutions abound but political will is in abeyance and has been for over four decades. The US government knew the climate dangers back in the 1970s, as did Exxon, but their adherence to profits-over-people economics has led to today's super-wicked dilemma: irrational policies disregard the future, those seeking to solve the problem also cause it, and time running out. That is plenty super-wicked, so much so that we may be fighting for what long-time activist Andrew Boyd calls a "better catastrophe."[1]

The key is fighting, or putting up the good fight no matter where we end up: an eventual thriving Anthropocene or picking up the pieces after collapse or something else. A thriving Anthropocene is best, but we will likely only thrive if we evolve to an age of human humility, rather than dominance, marked by simple living in sympathy with all species.

This much is clear: *we need the active soul.*

Emerson and Thoreau, while champions of solitude and reflection, are exemplars of and called for the active soul. Or rather, they were active because they reflected deeply on the newly wicked problems emerging from the shift from agrarianism to industrialization. Emerson feared that the mechanization of humanity outpaces the humanization of the machine and Thoreau wondered whether we ride on trains or if trains ride upon us.[2]

The train ferried Emerson to numerous lyceum speeches and Thoreau made use of rail travel when taking excursions outside of their hometown of Concord, Massachusetts. Thoreau also toured a locomotive factory and, spurred by his engineering skill that improved machinery for his family's pencil business, he wanted to examine every part and learn how to make one himself.[3] They both experienced the benefits of new technologies and saw positive possibilities, but they also saw the downsides, with Thoreau warning against "pretty toys" that are "improved means to unimproved ends."[4]

Emerson and Thoreau are worth studying for their response to the burgeoning techno-industrial capitalist world, as well as the intolerable and seemingly intractable institution that fueled it: slavery. Their abolitionist work is the focus of the essays and speeches in this volume. By exploring that work, we also find the roots of today's intolerable and seemingly intractable injustices, including climate injustice fueled by environmental racism. Marginalized peoples who have contributed the least to rising greenhouse gases are being affected the most.

In his 2020 article "Racism is Killing the Planet," Hop Hopkins reviews the link between social and ecological crises. The long intertwining history of racism and ecological destruction in the U.S. began with the genocide of Native Americans and land theft, with both justified by the narratives of Manifest Destiny and white superiority, and then "progressed" to slavery, once again justified by white superiority.[5] This story of dehumanization continues with the pollution and poisons generated by neoliberal economics disproportionately disposed on people of color and the poor who are considered disposable. To mention but a few examples: the Navajo Nation poisoned by uranium mining; Cancer Alley in Louisiana, also known as Death Alley; and polluted water in Flint, Michigan. Sacrifice zones mean that people are being sacrificed; if you cannot have sacrifice zones, then racism is abated.

No one deserves to be poisoned by uranium or live in Cancer Alley or have lead in their water, and Dakota Sioux did not deserve to have a pipeline built through their land, threatening their water supply, after it was rejected by white neighbors. And so the good fight continues, or as Thoreau put it in "Civil Disobedience," we must "make ourselves a counter-friction to stop the machine."

But what does effective counter-friction activism look like? Do we fight for reform of existing institutions, more radical change, or for both? Do we start with changing ourselves or society or both? What are the best strategies and tactics for changing lifeways and structures? What rhetoric is most persuasive? Is violence ever a proper response to violence? Does turning to violence lead to the loss of the moral high ground? How should we define violence? How can we pursue the ethical good while putting up the good fight?

Emerson and Thoreau do not have final answers to these questions. No one does: they are ongoing questions that need ongoing and always renewed responses. But there are plenty of lessons to be learned from the writings and actions of Emerson and Thoreau, who delved deeply into these questions by applying transcendentalist principles to the abolitionist cause. We need to mine those lessons if we are to fittingly respond to our Anthropocene angst and call forth a better future.

Transcendentalism is considered the first intellectual movement in the U.S., its heyday a brief decade between the mid-1830s and 1840s. Early transcendentalists first met in Boston, and then Concord, home of the first Revolutionary War battle and prior home to native Algonquians. Or more precisely, they met at Emerson's home, leading scholar Lawrence Buell to argue that transcendentalism was "an outpouring of radiant energy" instead of "an organized enterprise."[6] That energy was rooted in philosophical idealism, but they did not discuss ideas detached from the world; they were concerned with how religion, philosophy, and literature influenced social and political life. Their transcendentalist vision, extolling the higher law of unity-in-diversity, self-reliance, and conscience in pursuit of freedom, led to radical activities in the abolitionist movement, as well as the women's movement, Native American rights, elementary education, journalism, labor, and at Brook Farm, a short-lived eco-socialist commune.

Buell states that the transcendentalists most certainly did not easily agree, but they did have "a broadly shared conviction" in the infinitude of the individual and thus human potential. This conviction acted as an "intense and adaptable burning lens for incinerating orthodoxies on multiple fronts." They believed in an "universal human nature" as ground, albeit an evolving ground, for reform and civil disobedience.[7]

This volume begins with Emerson's seemingly tame "The Over-Soul." "Over-Soul" may sound like an odd term but it harkens back to Plato's conception of a world soul and the anima mundi pondered by many philosophers, in which everything is inspirited and alive. "The Over-Soul" explores the universal soul and thus universal human nature and transcendentalist principles that drove Emerson and Thoreau, and the transcendentalists generally, toward reform or radical action. But reform versus radicalism, while often encompassing different strategies and tactics, is a bit of a false dichotomy in their hands. What matters most is being active souls, and thus we would do well to have an understanding of the meaning of "soul," especially since the word can devolve into mealy-mouthed do-gooderism disconnected from larger forces. For Emerson, "soul" is a larger force. Or rather, individual soul connected to collective Over-Soul is a dynamic and mysterious force that seeks expression in the world: "Ineffable is the union of man and God in every act of the soul."[8]

Emerson's conception of soul, and God for that matter, follows the mystical dictum of "One in many, many in One." Out of that unity-in-diversity flows principled actions: "When it [the Over-Soul] breathes through his intellect, it is genius; when it breathes through his will, it is virtue; when it flows through his affection, it is love…. All reform aims in some one particular to have its way through us; in other words, to engage us to obey."[9]

"The Over-Soul" was published in 1841 along with another seminal essay, "Self-Reliance," which some scholars consider to be an ode to apolitical individualism, or worse, selfish individualism in which we do not conform to any social norm.[10] But self-reliance is best understood as radical inner listening that leads to reform of self but also society. The self-reliant individual is compelled to work for a democracy of the self-reliant.

For Emerson, personal change and societal change are intimately linked, but he begins with the individual attuned to Over-Soul. This self-reliant individual recognizes higher law and thus fights for principles that express universal human nature, including equality (the Over-Soul shines within all equally), rights (the Over-Soul accords all with dignity), and freedom (the Over-Soul's flourishing must not be denied or blocked by societal institutions). The pursuit of equality, rights, and freedom act as catalysts for the pursuit of justice.

Emerson was the epitome of the public intellectual and lecturer, and his influence was considerable. He did not speak merely to inform but to provoke individual reform, which then extended to reform of society. But, again, such reform only has value if it resonates with Over-Soul and is practiced by attending to the divine within ourselves and all things. He most certainly was not in favor of reform for the sake of reform, giving the speeches "Man the Reformer" in 1841 and "New England Reformers" in 1844 that acknowledge humankind's propensity and potential for reform while making distinctions among actions that elicit soul and those that do not.

We are born "to be a Reformer," he exhorted, "a "Remaker of what man has made; a renouncer of lies; a restorer of truth and good, imitating that great Nature that embosoms us all..."[11] The key to worthwhile reform is imitating that great Nature, which is another way of saying obeying, or following, the dictates of Over-Soul. This higher law expression of unity, and thus love, out in the world is a high standard, but those who live up to it "make it easier for all who follow him, to go in honor, and with benefit."[12]

In the Introduction to *A Political Companion to Ralph Waldo Emerson*, editors Alan M. Levine and Daniel S. Malachuk argue that Emerson's advocacy evolved in stages. In the first stage, during his late twenties as a Unitarian minister, he advocated for self-reliance expressed as "moral suasion." Such moral suasion should be rooted in reason, or spiritual intuitions of the Over-Soul, not just our understanding defined as material calculation or empiricism. In a 1932 sermon, for example, he argued that such reasoning results in revelatory ethics rooted in unity: "Let every man say then to himself—the cause of the Indian, it is mine, the cause of the slave, it is mine; the cause of the union, it is mine; the cause of public honesty, of education, of religion, they are mine."[13]

According to Levine and Malachuk, early abolitionists practiced moral suasion via a variety of tactics, including organizing lectures, clubs, associations, and societies; publishing pamphlets and newspapers; petitioning local, state, and federal governments; and speaking out in town hall meetings, with Emerson participating in all of them. In his second stage, however, Emerson expressed doubts about moral suasion's effectiveness. This concern was heightened in 1838 when southern Cherokee were forcefully relocated beyond the Mississippi River in the horrific "Trail of Tears." Emerson's wife, Lidian, urged him to write a letter to then-president Martin Van Buren on behalf of the Cherokee, which he did but to no avail.[14]

For Emerson, the town hall was less and less effective; it was increasingly becoming a vehicle of conformity rather than soul and self-reliance. Or, as he stated in "New England Reformers," "society gains nothing whilst a man, not himself renovated, attempts to renovate things around him...."[15] He was also concerned about fiery abolitionists, who, while aware of the cause might not be self-aware. He feared they might be caught up in ego-activism that props up a self-image rather than practicing soul-activism that leads to genuine reform. To him, there is a big difference between not doing self-work while attempting to impose reform on others and being self-reliant and making a contribution to lasting change.[16]

Emerson was further concerned with single issue politics, arguing that everything must be reformed: "Do not be so vain of your one objection. Do you think there is only one? Alas! My good friend, there is no part of society or of life better than any other part. All our things are right and wrong together. The wave of evil washes all our institutions alike." Emerson sought "total regeneration" and, it would seem, coalition politics and intersectionality, in which injustices share the same source and thus we must share in each other's causes.[17]

His doubts about moral suasion as a vehicle for reform took on added import and urgency when he began to more fully confront slavery in the 1840s. Slavery, of course, attempts to nullify the Over-Soul and negate self-reliance, but, since soul attuned to Soul is an unending immaterial force, it continually arises as the pursuit of equality, rights, freedom, and justice. And if that pursuit is negated, it rises as increased radicalism and civil disobedience.

Levine and Malachuk argue he vacillated between an ecstatic liberalism that championed individual and societal potential when Over-Soul is expressed and sober liberalism that perceived structural blocks to actualizing this potential.[18] He was also trying to figure out what role to play, or how he could serve his constitution, his genius, and the cause. The best case scenario is to do both, or, as the twentieth-century theologian Frederick Buechner put it, God calls us to find the place where our "deep gladness and the world's deep hunger meet." This is a beautiful ideal but there is often a tension between the call of personal vocation and the call of the world. To Emerson, we inevitably make a contribution by being self-reliant, but he was playing out that tension. Being an activist should be a true vocation.

Emerson's appeal to ecstatic liberalism, or ecstasy, which was one of his favorite words, was another way for him to privilege divine revelation and adherence to higher law over human-made law, which he made clear in his 1851 and 1854 "The Fugitive Slave Law" speeches: "no forms, neither constitutions, nor laws, nor covenants, nor churches, nor bibles, are any use in themselves. The Devil nestles comfortably into them all."[19] Slavery was anathema to Emerson's vision of a democracy of self-reliant individuals. The active soul abhors injustice and is compelled to engage the good fight no matter the circumstance. Thus, he entered a third stage of advocating for reform via consistent support for abolitionism.

Emerson wrote a new, and often fiery, attack denouncing slavery nearly every year between 1844 and 1863 and delivered them over and over to the public. He still practiced moral suasion but amped up the volume, both in rhetoric and frequency, by criticizing the legitimacy of the government and supporting direct action. Emerson was more optimistic and hopeful in early speeches thanks to his heartfelt belief in universal human potential but became less so as slavery continued to disclose the depths of human depravity. He realized that "total regeneration" reform and individual action were not working, and so he started to support abolitionist associations and organized efforts, moving from poet-scholar to poet-scholar-reformer. The abolitionist cause began to override his gentle and sometimes aloof constitution and added new elements to his character. Or rather, his constitution expanded by confronting the evils of his time.[20]

Thoreau's "Civil Disobedience" was published in 1849, two years before Emerson's "The Fugitive Slave Law" speech, which leads one to wonder: Did Thoreau's rhetoric influence Emerson's? Thoreau was fourteen years younger than Emerson and was mentored by him. In Buell's *Henry David Thoreau: Thinking Disobediently*, he argues that Thoreau followed Emerson's areas of inquiry: "Nature, Self-Reliance, Experience, Heroism, Higher Laws, Politics, Reform."[21] This is not surprising given Emerson's mentorship and the fact that these are key themes of transcendentalism and their times. But Thoreau always gave his unique spin, which was often more radical.

In "Civil Disobedience," Thoreau tells the story of his refusal to pay a poll tax for six years, a protest against the government's support of slavery and war with Mexico, but also the removal of Native Americans from their land. He spent a night in jail—it would have been more but his aunt bailed him out, to his chagrin—and the result was his well-known claim: "Under a government which imprisons any unjustly, the true place for a just man is also a prison." But this story often includes the fable that Emerson passed by the jail and supposedly said, "what are you doing in there," to which Thoreau replied: "what are you doing out there?"[22] While this event never happened, it illustrates differences in character and constitution, with Emerson cautioning against extremism while Thoreau argued, "I know of few radicals as yet who are radical enough."[23]

Thoreau was a living example of self-reliance, or, as Emerson put it, he "gives me, in flesh and blood…my own ethics."[24] For Thoreau, such self-reliant ethics are expressed by following conscience, which is the central argument of "Civil Disobedience." Following conscience is the only way to freely serve the State. Politicians and other professionals tend to serve with their heads only, making them poor in ethical decisions. They patronize virtue instead of living virtuously, as they are sold to institutions that make them rich, beholden to free trade instead of true freedom. On the other hand, Thoreau greatly respected the courage of the soldier, who served with their bodies, but argued that they often march counter to head, heart, and ethical sense. True heroes and patriots, then, serve their conscience expressed outwardly in the pursuit of justice. Such citizens are friends of the State but often treated as enemies.

Thoreau understood that the machinery of government can't be perfect, that there is a degree of injustice in its workings, but if this makes us an agent of injustice against another, conscience demands that we make ourselves a counter-friction. Conscience, of course, is linked to the Over-Soul and the higher law of unity-in-diversity. The Bible and Constitution are great documents, he argued, but they are not the final word, especially since seemingly good-hearted humans have used them to justify what should not be justified. Thoreau was always critical of individual conformity and mistrustful of societal institutions and many reform efforts.[25] The higher law expressed as virtue ethics, on the other hand, acts as justification for taking action, including principled law-breaking.[26]

The rhetoric in "Civil Disobedience" is plenty strong, but he made it stronger in his speech "Slavery in Massachusetts." He did so for good reason. When 20-year-old Anthony Burns was captured and tried in Boston in 1854 in accord with the Fugitive Slave Law of 1850, Thoreau wrote in his journal that it was actually Massachusetts on trial: "every moment that she hesitates to set this man free—she is convicted." Inspired by Frederick Douglass and Wendell Phillips, a transcendentalist pastor and abolitionist orator, he soon gave his "Slavery in Massachusetts" address before a crowd estimated to be as high as 2000 in Boston in July 4th heat. He spoke of living for months with a feeling of "vast infinite loss," unsure what it was, and then realizing: "At last it occurred to me that what I had lost was a country." Running with this theme, he continued, "My thoughts are murder to the State, and involuntarily go plotting against her."[27]

Thoreau's remarks were revolutionary, including calling for secession from the union. He had become a radical abolitionist and his address was soon run in newspapers, with one using the headline "Words that Burn." Emerson also increasingly used strong rhetoric, stating "we must get rid of slavery, or we must get rid of freedom."[28] Fully into his third stage, he called for collective direct action because we cannot practice self-reliance if we are not free. But to the public, Thoreau's burning words freed him from Emerson's shadow. The defender of nature and proponent of simple living had joined Frederick Douglass and others in declaring that the Declaration of Independence was a lie.[29]

Thoreau's rhetoric soared in his defense of captured slaves. It is hard to imagine it soaring further, but then came his defense of John Brown. Brown, along with his followers, murdered five proslavery householders in Kansas. At first blush, it is also hard to imagine Thoreau or anyone supporting such acts—one biographer questioned whether he knew about this grisly event[30]—but the murders, known as the Pottawatomie Massacre, were in retaliation for the sacking of Lawrence, Kansas by pro-slavery forces, who destroyed the presses of two abolitionist newspapers and burnt down the "Free State Hotel," used as an abolitionist home base. Brown was angered by this aggression, but also because no anti-slavery force defended the town. He was further angered when he heard that Charles Sumner, an abolitionist senator, was nearly beaten to death on the senate floor by a southern congressperson.[31]

Brown was fed up and willing to fight back. But we should be clear about this: Brown and his followers, including his sons, did not kill in battle, but at night and in cold-blood by raiding three separate cabins. He soon traveled east, including to Concord, dining at the Thoreau home and staying at the Emersons', and then gave a speech at a town meeting to raise funds for the abolitionist movement. Thoreau was impressed by his passion, even though Brown advocated for violence in response to violence.[32]

After Brown's imprisonment due to his failed raid on the federal arsenal at Harper's Ferry, Virginia, Thoreau stewed, and then, two days after hearing the news of Brown's capture, passed the word among fellow townsfolk he would speak. Friends and some family begged for silence. He replied to one friend, Franklin Sanborn the schoolmaster, who had been involved in Brown's plot and now feared for his life: "I did not send for you for advice but to announce that I am to speak." Brown was on trial for treason, newspapers denounced him, and Thoreau was the first to stand up in public to defend him. The church was filled to capacity, and Thoreau read his essay, "A Plea for Captain John Brown," before a curious but doubtful audience, with "no oratory, as if it burned him." Young Edward Emerson, Ralph Waldo's son, said he sounded like he was speaking about his own brother, and summarized the reaction: "Many of those who came to scoff remained to pray."[33]

Word spread, thanks to Emerson, who lent his authority as a nationally known figure to Brown's cause. When Frederick Douglass, scheduled to speak in Boston, was implicated in the plot by a letter found on Brown, a warrant was put out for his arrest and he was forced to flee to Canada; Thoreau stepped in before a crowd of 2500: "The reason why Frederick Douglass is not here is the reason why I am," he began, the audience rapt and applauding. An abridged "Plea" was printed in newspapers across America; he hoped to get it published as a pamphlet but no publisher would touch it.[34]

Thoreau planned a memorial service on the day of Brown's execution; many in Concord were against Brown and not happy about it. Thoreau later helped Francis Jackson Merriam, a Harper's Ferry plotter and financial supporter, and the most wanted man in America, to escape to Canada, although his identity was supposedly unknown to him. It is hard to imagine he did not know, with Thoreau putting himself at great risk, potentially jailed and hanged himself for aiding a fugitive.[35]

Spurred by Brown, Thoreau's position on nonviolence and violence evolved; he refused to judge "any tactics that are effective of good, whether one wields the quill or sword."[36] He most certainly entered difficult terrain here. Prominent abolitionists like William Garrison had vowed to only use nonviolent tactics; but, for Thoreau, any rebuke of Brown must consider the crimes of a country that institutionalized the violent enslavement of four million fellow Americans. And while turning ideas into actions marked the transcendentalist call to conscience, Thoreau showed that words are actions when they drive a wedge into institutions. In his 1860 speech and essay, "The Last Days of John Brown," given nine months after "Plea," he stated that "The North is suddenly all Transcendental," giving him hope in the power of words and ideals and speaking the truth: the government was on the wrong side, hanging those that would liberate the slave.

In "The Last Days," Thoreau argued that Brown was a transcendentalist above all, revering higher law over law and embodying principle and conscience. If anti-Brown citizens were Christians, they were neither citizen nor Christian, having no genius for listening to inner light or being a free man: "They seem to have known nothing about living or dying for a principle." And that, for Thoreau, was the most profound lesson of John Brown: The public now had an example of living and dying for principle. Thoreau, staying true to conscience, wondered how he could do more: "I do not wish to kill or to be killed, but I can foresee circumstances in which both of these things would be by me unavoidable."[37]

Emerson did not mirror this rhetoric, but he continued to speak passionately in his "The Fugitive Slave Law" addresses, the first in Concord and the second at a church in Manhattan before a crowd of over 2000 in 1854. He then followed this address with a new one, "Lecture on Slavery," which he first delivered in 1855 in Boston and then would deliver at least seven more times in major cities. Emerson signaled his more radical shift by stating, "One must write with a red hot iron to make any impression" and "It is so delicious to act with great masses to great aims."[38] He knew he needed to speak in hard words to be heard and further extolled his believe that self-reliant individualism and communal action go hand in hand.

Brown's turn to violence alienated many, but Thoreau was having none of it, calling the government a brute force while questioning what citizens were willing to do. Like

Emerson, his activist response to slavery evolved in stages. In "Civil Disobedience," he mostly advocates for nonviolence while stating that the Constitution is a fallback for those unable to follow higher law and conscience; in "Slavery in Massachusetts," he advocates for burning the Constitution; and in his John Brown speeches and essays, he's open to justified violence against an unjust State and unjust laws. In "A Plea for Captain John Brown," he states most think that rifles and revolvers are righteously used for duels, or when "insulted by other nations, or to hunt Indians, or shoot fugitive slaves," but only Brown "employed" them in a "righteous cause."[39]

Did Thoreau's praise and support for John Brown go too far? Did his rhetoric veer into hagiography? For sure, Thoreau, and Emerson, helped turn him into a martyr. Thoreau saw that Brown's raid, while unsuccessful in its immediate goal, could successfully serve the larger goal of stoking outrage and tipping the abolitionist scales. He sought to turn Brown into more than a fallen hero; he became an idea, or a transcendentalist ideal, that could be used to further drive a wedge into the institution of slavery. That wedge would lead to the Civil War. In 1861, with Thoreau's health worsening due to a long bout with tuberculosis, the War would begin when Confederate troops fired on Fort Sumter in South Carolina. He would die in 1862 at 44, and thus the country lost his vigilant voice.

Emerson supported the Civil War because Lincoln had linked it to emancipation. He saw it as an inevitable path to finally ending slavery. While touring a Charleston Navy Yard, he even reportedly said, "Gunpowder sometimes smells good." That is a far cry from where he began in the late 1830s, with his wife Lidian nudging him into the cause.

In his scathing 1851 "Fugitive Slave Law" speech he still considered the possible solution of the government paying Southern slaveholders for their "property." By the time of the war, he argued that the only one deserving to be paid were slaves for their years of backbreaking labor.[40]

Thoreau and Emerson were certainly not the only ones espousing fiery rhetoric. Their support of John Brown occurred within the context of abolitionism becoming more popular and increased resistance. In *Fighting for the Higher Law*, Peter Wirzbicki catalogues that resistance from white and especially black transcendentalists. Wirzbicki writes that transcendentalism, as philosophy, and abolitionism, as politics, were "mutually reinforcing" and "helped create each other." Abolitionism grounded transcendentalist principles in action, but abolitionist activism needed moral grounding to reach the public and be effective. This mutuality extended to black and white transcendentalists and activists working together for their common cause.[41]

Frederick Douglass is a prominent example. In 1852, he gave his famous "What to the Slave Is the Fourth of July" speech, which forcefully reminds that this "glorious anniversary" for celebrating independence "only reveals the immeasurable distance between us." What brought justice and liberty and prosperity to whites (or white males), brought injustice and cruelty and death to blacks: "You may rejoice, I must mourn."[42] In another memorable speech in 1857, he spoke on the "philosophy of reform": "Those who profess to favor freedom and yet deprecate agitation, are men who want crops without plowing up the ground, they want rain without thunder and lightning. They want the ocean without the awful roar of the waters. This struggle may be a moral one, or it may be a physical one, and it may be both moral and physical, but it must be a struggle." Douglass searingly summed up his call for revolutionary reform: "Power concedes nothing without a demand. It never has and it never will."[43]

Douglass worked with the Massachusetts Anti-Slavery Society and gave an untold number of speeches over many years in small towns, often staying the night with friendly supporters after confronting unfriendly crowds. During an 1844 stop in Northampton, he stayed with a utopian socialist community and encountered genuine expressions of equality, including Sojourner Truth working side by side with white men and women. But there are plenty of lesser-known figures who fought the good fight, including William C. Nell, a black transcendentalist, who participated in teaching "conversations" with the white transcendentalist Bronson Alcott (a friend of Emerson and Thoreau and father of Louisa May), and the black doctor and activist John S. Rock, who debated race and racism with the transcendentalist minister Theodore Parker.[44]

An especially dramatic example is the black transcendentalist and activist Lewis Hayden, the principal organizer of the Boston Vigilance Committee, who worked with other black activists and white transcendentalists to protect the escaped slaves William and Ellen Craft. When slavecatchers empowered by the "legalities" of the Fugitive Slave Law arrived to return the Crafts to their "owners," they were confronted by a group of armed black activists ready to fight. Hayden threatened to ignite a barrel of gunpowder with a torch and blow up the whole block rather than hand over any runaway slave. The slavecatchers left and the Crafts made their way to England and began giving antislavery speeches.[45]

Wirzbicki writes that black intellectuals and activists pushed white transcendentalists to take bolder stances, with all following the "Higher Law Ethos." This bolder stance was rooted in their experience of racism, not just the idea of it, and the willingness to use violence in response to violence. Like Emerson and Thoreau, black intellectuals also wrote books or pamphlets and gave lectures. White transcendentalists did not always show black transcendentalists mutual regard, but they attended each other's clubs, participated in shared teaching conversations, raised money together, and, in some instances, turned to physical violence and bled together.[46]

When Anthony Burns was jailed, black abolitionists, again led by Hayden, and white abolitionists, led by the transcendentalist Thomas Wentworth Higginson, joined forces to break him out. They rushed the door but were greeted by US marshals swinging clubs. Higginson received a deep wound on his chin, a marshal was shot dead (Hayden later admitted to the deed), and Burns was not rescued. In hindsight, the timing of the plan was off: many of the abolitionists arrived too late to make a difference. Thoreau would deliver his "Slavery in Massachusetts" address soon after, most assuredly influenced by the incident.[47]

The abolitionist stakes were raised day after day, month after month, year after year, and Emerson and Thoreau made significant contributions. But as Wirzbicki makes clear, they were two of many fighting the good fight. This includes many women, such as Margaret Fuller, the author of *Woman in the Nineteenth Century* and editor of the transcendentalist journal *The Dial* (among numerous other accomplishments). For Fuller, abolitionism and women's rights were twin causes, with men too much under the slavery of habit. And while Lidian was a catalyst for Emerson's social and activist conscience, Thoreau was shaped by his mother and sisters, who were members of the Concord Female Anti-Slavery Society. The Society led men into the cause, and the Thoreau household, run by his strong-willed mother, Cynthia, sheltered runaway slaves as part of Underground Railroad, with Thoreau helping to escort them to safety. His sister, Helen, worked with Frederick Douglass and William Lloyd Garrison, the publisher of *The Liberator*, an abolitionist newspaper, before Thoreau was drawn into the fight.[48]

Emerson and Thoreau also influenced, and aided, each other. In 1844, Emerson, along with Douglass, were set to give speeches in Concord on the anniversary of the abolition of slavery in the British West Indies. The event was organized by Female Anti-Slavery members, including Helen, but they ran into a problem: the minister of the First Parish Church, where they hoped to meet, refused them entrance because he was angered by their call for disunion. Rain kept them from holding the event outside, and so they moved it to the courthouse, but no one was willing to ring the First Parish bell to call the community together. Thoreau pushed through bystanders and happily rang it, gathering a large crowd for Emerson's first more radical foray into speaking out against the scourge of slavery. Thoreau would further aid Emerson by getting the speech distributed as a pamphlet.[49]

Emerson and Thoreau were not perfect, of course. Despite being virulently antislavery in writings and speeches, Emerson was not above the idea of superiority in his 1856 book *English Traits*, although he also countered this idea in parts of the book and many speeches, including his "British West Indies" speech, where he extolled equality and countered the claim that blacks were inferior. It was a strong and passionate lecture on reform, a big success with his abolitionist audience, and led him to bond with leading abolitionists.[50] Still, Nell Irvin Painter analyzes his over-the-top racial bias toward Anglo-Saxon heritage in her book, *The History of White People*. This bias says something about Emerson, but it says even more about race theory during his time. Such views were widespread, including among abolitionists.

Thoreau seemed to have escaped this bias, but despite his study of, experience with, and high regard for Native Americans, in some journal entries he fell prey to the myth of savagery. Or rather, in many ways he saw Natives, and Native lifeways, as superior, but because of his extensive study of Native American ethnology, which was buried in the bias of inferiority, he struggled at times to transcend his times.[51]

Emerson's seeming slowness to fully join the abolitionist fight, at least compared to other transcendentalists, has also been criticized. But his unfolding stages were honest attempts to find his voice and as such they deserve respect. At first, he was more sympathetic observer than advocate. He mostly stayed on the sidelines, despite long despising slavery, based on his self-reliant constitution that skewed towards intellectual discussion and education. He was wisely hesitant to join any crowd without sufficient reflection, especially given his heartfelt believe that outer change is not lasting without inner change.

Thoreau also resisted getting involved in politics; not only because he was drawn to self-reliance and going his own way, but because he was drawn to nature. On the other hand, his discoveries in nature—unity-in-diversity, wild freedom, and living virtuously—drove him to respond to injustice. In *Thoreau's Religion*, Alda Bathrop-Lewis argues that Thoreau is often put into separate boxes, the nature lover and the antislavery activist, when the two are actually one because they come from the same place: his transcendentalist world view and spiritual practices. Those practices included inner listening and listening to nature's diverse voices, which put him into right relationship with the nonhuman but also the human world.[52]

To Bathrop-Lewis, Thoreau was a political ascetic, especially when staying at Walden Pond. By giving up luxuries and living a disciplined life, he was better able to pursue the true, good, and beautiful. Seeking solace in nature is not an escape, but a pilgrimage to an energizing force that invigorates the body, clears the mind, and propels the soul to fight for what is worth preserving in the world. And going his own way was a form of politics; he was often led by what he refused to do. Or, as he wrote in "Civil Disobedience," conscience demands that we do what "belongs" to us and "the hour."[53]

The Fugitive Slave Law of 1850 was the incendiary "hour" that changed everything for both Emerson and Thoreau. When Thomas Sims, a young runaway with an unknown birthday, was sent back to Georgia under the Act on April 12, 1851, a week before a planned celebration of the freedom fought for in the battles of Lexington and Concord on April 19, 1775, Thoreau was horrified by the hypocrisy, referencing Jesus: "inasmuch as ye did it unto the least of these his brethren ye did it unto him. Do you think *he* would have stayed here in liberty and let the black man go in slavery in his stead?"[54] Emerson, too, had reached his limit, appalled, and thus called by conscience to speak out two weeks later: "The last year has forced us all into politics." He also mirrored Thoreau's strong rhetoric in "Civil Disobedience": "An immoral law makes it a man's duty to break it, at every hazard."[55]

Despite being somewhat slow to get fully involved in the fight, Emerson and Thoreau are not as they have often been depicted: a removed scholar in his study and a removed hermit living at Walden Pond. That depiction not only does an injustice to them, but undermines the pursuit of justice, especially racial justice. Emerson is much easier to deal with if he is just a bookish sage and Thoreau is easier to deal with if he just hangs out in the woods and communes with wildlife. Both were defanged via popular myths and misreadings of self-reliant individualism. Emerson was a man of the people and Thoreau was a townie intimately involved in his community. They were active souls passionate about social change and willing to put their reputations and bodies on the line.

Emerson and Thoreau's active soul accomplishments are many. Along with Emerson's abundant and authoritative writings and a staggering amount of speeches (approximately 1500 over the course of his life), he attended abolitionist meetings, wrote letters, pushed petitions, refused to speak if there was segregated seating, donated money to freeing escaped slaves, supported antislavery politicians, supported the most radical abolitionist voices, and was the leading intellectual figure of his time.[56] Along with Thoreau's abundant and authoritative writings and speeches (a far less staggering but still impressive and influential 75 or so), he championed and practiced simple living counter to the materialist mainstream, ferried escaped slaves and white abolitionist lawbreakers via the Underground Railroad, stayed put and embraced the local commons, including by helping farmers to better understand their land, and was an ahead-of-his-time ecologist who integrated science with poetic feeling while recording massive amounts of data on flower blossoming that current scientists are using to study climate change.[57]

Emerson and Thoreau are also leading figures in the history of transcendentalism. And transcendentalism, with Emerson calling for an original relation to the universe, especially inspired and influenced the young, beginning a tradition of "countercultural movements."[58]

All of these accomplishments, and more, influenced their own time, but also ensuing years and decades and centuries. Emerson met with President Lincoln twice, as well as the U.S. Secretary of State, William H. Seward, and was read by industrialists such as Andrew Carnegie and William H. Forbes (whose son married Emerson's youngest daughter).[59] He was also revered by and influenced Walt Whitman, along with untold other writers. Of course, he was criticized and misread but he has been a steady presence in the history of American literature and thought. Living longer and being famous gave him more influence than Thoreau during their time, but Thoreau's life and writings have become a growing historical presence, and in many ways he has outshined his mentor, including influencing the modern environmental movement. In particular, "Civil Disobedience" inspired Leo Tolstoy, Mahatma Gandhi, and Martin Luther King, Jr.

One can clearly see the higher law ethos expressed in King's life and many speeches and writings. "Letter from a Birmingham Jail" is a powerful example of the higher law in action, especially since he lived Thoreau's argument that jail is the only place for a just citizen in an unjust society. The "Letter" is filled with active soul rhetoric, such as "Injustice anywhere is a threat to justice everywhere" and "freedom is never voluntarily given by the oppressor; it must be demanded by the oppressed." King supplies four steps for activism: gathering facts to confirm the existence of injustice, the willingness to negotiate, self-purification to make sure one is acting out of conscience, and then direct action. It would be great if negotiation alleviated factually confirmed injustices, but when negotiation is refused, nonviolent civil disobedience based in conscience is needed to restart negotiation and compel real change. Such civil disobedience includes breaking unjust laws that do not mirror higher law, or what King called "moral law" and "eternal law."[60]

Emerson and Thoreau's ongoing influence is incalculable. They spoke to King and 1960s civil rights and anti-Vietnam War activism, and they speak to us today, and will speak to future "todays" because they appeal to the universal; or rather, they have universal appeal because they appeal to principles that have evolving universal resonance. Their criticisms of institutions birthed at the beginnings of the Anthropocene add to that appeal and make them increasingly relevant as eco-social ills multiply and magnify with each fraction of a degree of warming. All were driven into politics in their time because of slavery; all are increasingly being driven into politics in our climate crisis times.

Slavery and climate are not equivalent crises. In *What We're Fighting for Now is Each Other: Dispatches from the Front Lines of Climate Justice,* Wen Stephenson writes that nothing compares to "the enslavement, systemic torture, and mass murder of countless human beings on the basis of race." However, he also points out salient similarities: enormous moral, human, and economic stakes; fierce and powerful opposition to doing what is right (the antebellum South and today's fossil fuel lobby); and the fight for equality, rights, freedom, and justice, including economic justice. Most importantly, climate crisis needs an equivalent movement inspired by spiritual principles.[61]

There are many lessons to glean from the past if we are to better respond to our present. Or, as William Faulkner wrote: "The past is never dead. It is not even past." We are still living out the Civil War in the culture wars. We are still living out the fallout from an economic system that exploits people and planet. We are still living out deeply rooted racism expressed as climate injustice. We are also still living out the question of nonviolence versus violence as a response to violence.

Erica Chenoweth, a scholar of civil disobedience, argues from her research that every nonviolent movement in the twentieth century with at least 3.5% of the population involved met with political success.⁶² On the other hand, Andreas Malm, in *How to Blow Up a Pipeline*, argues that those successful nonviolent movements were supported by the threat of violence and strategic violence against property, which Chenoweth ignores in her analysis.⁶³

Malm's book sounds like an instruction manual when it's actually a nuanced exploration of social movement strategies and tactics. He gives numerous historical examples, including British suffragettes, who, after many years of unsuccessful negotiation with Parliament, finally got fed up and turned to radical tactics: breaking lots of windows, setting letterboxes on fire, throwing stones, dousing the Prime Minister with pepper, fighting with police, and an ongoing campaign of arson, among other militant acts. They also hosted huge rallies, owned presses, and went on hunger strikes, and thus their strategy was a mix of nonviolence and violence against property. No person was ever hurt, but they did everything they could to hurt the system that prevented them from having the right to vote.⁶⁴

Emerson and Thoreau had a deeply-held disposition toward nonviolence. Yet, both virulently supported John Brown, and Emerson welcomed the Civil War and Thoreau could imagine himself being willing to kill or be killed. King, of course, also had a deeply-held disposition toward nonviolence, and yet Malm cites an example of a journalist visiting him at his parsonage after his house had been bombed and finding a chair with loaded guns—King said the guns were for self-defense. Malm also cites the example of King, once again in jail, warning that if nonviolence did not work, more militant forces, and more militant leaders, like Malcom X, would rise in influence. This is the radical flank effect, in which a more militant faction makes other factions more mainstream and more appealing. To Malm, it was once again the mixing of nonviolence with the threat of violence, and some violence, that was most effective, leading to the Civil Rights Act of 1964.[65]

Like with Emerson and Thoreau's support of Brown, we have entered dangerous ground here. These are difficult questions to wrestle with, but wrestle with them we must because we have entered dangerous ground in the Anthropocene. Or, as Malm argues, we have entered completely new dangerous ground: climate crisis is such an overbearing and overarching global emergency that comparisons with the past might not be relevant.[66] And yet, the past is not even past and holds inspiring examples of the active soul responding to major crises. Whether that response should include situational violence of some type cannot be known in advance, and even in hindsight we are dealing with uncertainty and risk. But from the perspective of the Over-Soul we must make a distinction between revelations rooted in the principle of unity and impulses rooted in an aggrieved isolated ego and unattended shadow.

There is a huge difference between a conscious rage based in ethical principles and unconscious shadow-sides thirsting for blood and lashing out in violence. Or, to give a concrete example, there is a world of difference between the radicalism of soulful activists breaking unjust laws because they dwell within the higher law and pursue justice and the radicalism of right-wing Trump "MAGA" supporters breaking just laws due to falsehoods and alienation and unjustified anger in the January 6, 2021 attack on the Capitol. We live in perilous post-truth times of "alternative facts," which is another reason we must attune to Over-Soul: we get closer to truth when following ethical principles of unity and love. Or, when unity and love are denied, so is truth, and so we must fight on behalf of and embody unity and love.

In a *New York Times* guest essay, "Trump Embraces Lawlessness, but in the Name of a Higher Law," Matthew Schmitz argues that Trump positions himself as an outsider and outlaw hero defending democratic values of freedom and justice (as defined by him). He claims the political, and legal, system that attacks him is corrupt, and so he can break the law and get away with it. He celebrates his lawlessness, turning vice into virtue. Due to the power of myth, it does not matter to many voters that none of this is based in fact.[67] But let's be clear: it is also not based in Over-Soul and higher law. He is not a present day John Brown following God and conscience. Again, there is a huge difference between soul-activism and ego-activism, or worse, the actions of an aggrieved narcissist who believes in the divine right of presidents.

We must also ask whether violence is already occurring with every increase in global warming, or heating, to use more accurate rhetoric. Is not rising CO_2 an act of violence when seen within the context of the Over-Soul and an interdependent ecosystem? In her 2019 speech to the UN, Greta Thunberg put it this way: "You have stolen my dreams and my childhood with your empty words. And yet I am one of the lucky ones. People are suffering. People are dying. Entire ecosystems are collapsing. We are in the beginning of a mass extinction, and all you can talk about is money and fairy tales of eternal economic growth. How dare you!" Thunberg ended her speech with a mix of challenge and threat: "We will not let you get away with this. Right here, right now is where we draw the line. The world is waking up. And change is coming, whether you like it not."[68]

An enlightening exercise would be to compare the rhetoric of Emerson and Thoreau with the rhetoric of Thunberg, who is carrying on a civil disobedience and call to conscience tradition. It would also be an enlightening exercise to compare their rhetoric with the rhetoric of radical right-wingers, or left-wingers, or any political persuasion. Emerson and Thoreau amped it up and spoke in hard words to be heard amid the deadly din of slavery, and their words reflected the fire of soul and the pursuit of rights, equality, freedom, and justice. I repeat it again because it makes all the difference: that fire and those pursuits are governed by Over-Soul, or principles of unity and love and thus the fact that we live in relationship to others.

King referenced Martin Buber in "Letter from a Birmingham Jail," and Buber argued there are two fundamental expressions of relationship: I-Thou, in which we treat others like alive subjects (with soul) and I-It, in which we treat others like objects (no soul).[69] As much as possible, activism should be rooted in the former and eschew the latter. Said differently, the Over-Soul expressed as I-Thou relations should be the measure. Here is an easy test: does a government, or president or leader, or corporation, treat others like Thous or Its? If the former, we are on our way to a more just world but must continue the good fight; if the latter, the good fight includes making ourselves a counter-friction to stop the machine.

But even when we treat others like Thous, the politics of policy is often messy and hard. And so is the politics of activism. Can we treat someone as a Thou and still commit violence? When is self-defense justified? When is self-defense writ large justified, like in response to the I-It institutions of slavery and fossil fuel climate injustice? These are the questions we need to ask. These are the questions that those who are not attuned to Over-Soul fail to ask.

Thunberg does not mention the Over-Soul but her criticisms of eternal economic growth are rooted in the eternal, or unfolding universal principles that we must embody in the now. Or, as Thoreau quipped: "As if you could kill time without injuring eternity" and "We should be blessed if we lived in the present always."[70] More recently, Thunberg and others, including many youth, have focused on climate justice, often getting removed from protests by police. In May 2024, she and other campaigners used an old fashioned sit-in to block entrance to Swedish Parliament in response to government inaction.

And so it goes, and so it will go for years to come. The rhetoric is getting amped up, the actions are getting amped up, at the same time as Malm and others question strategies and tactics while drawing on insights from the past. In 2023, Extinction Rebellion, the climate activist group and movement that has blocked roads, glued themselves to public spaces, thrown paint, and used other disruptive tactics, put out a document titled "We Quit." What they are quitting, though, is these disruptive tactics, not the good fight. After polling indicated they were losing too much public sympathy, they are changing strategy, focusing on "relationships over roadblocks" to grow the movement: "In a time when speaking out and taking action are criminalized, building collective power, strengthening in number and thriving through bridge-building is a radical act."[71] While the new strategy focuses on effectiveness, Extinction Rebellion leadership is responding to new laws that restrict protest and increase jail time. Extinction Rebellion also seeks to join forces with other activist groups, but some of those groups, such as Just Stop Oil, are increasing radical direct action.

Emerson's sober liberalism championed the freedom of individuals to disagree. We will most certainly not all agree, even when on the same side of political issues. We should follow his sage advice, which is especially salient in current culture wars: "Let me never fall into the vulgar mistake of dreaming that I am persecuted whenever I am contradicted."[72] But Emerson's ecstatic liberalism championed liberty for all, rooted in Over-Soul and love and justice, and thus slavery had to end. Some things are just wrong, and obviously so from the perspective of higher law. The same should be true of climate injustice. But dialogue is much-needed on how to end it, and that dialogue must also be guided by higher law and I-Thou relations.

For Emerson and Thoreau and many others, The Fugitive Slave Law was the kick in the ass that took calls for reform and civil disobedience to new levels. And then John Brown took the call to still newer levels. What will be our Fugitive Slave Law and John Brown moments? Many have already had their moments. Will we reach Chenoweth's 3.5% of the population taking it to the streets for nonviolence to be effective? Many have already become grassroots activists. But we need many more moments and activists.

Emerson admitted that slavery, while abhorrent, did not seem to touch him at first. But then it did. Of course, climate crisis does touch us—we are just not always cognizant and attuned to our senses unless it is in our faces: heat domes in the Pacific northwest, floods in Houston, wildfires in California, record-breaking heat in Phoenix, smoke drifting down from Canada and covering New York City. And that is just a few examples from the U.S. For starters, add the 2020 bushfires in Australia that burned 24 million hectares and killed up to 1.5 billion wild animals.

We are also not always attuned to the climate data and scientific consensus, including on planetary boundaries that we are already crossing, and we are not always attuned to higher law and the call for climate justice. What will it take for climate crisis and climate justice to touch us and make us active souls? How should we be active in a complicit world, in which we pollute by just driving to work? In "Civil Disobedience," Thoreau argued that we should not be complicit in slavery, or we should not add to the wrong, and that refusal is a sufficient response; but he also argued that when the State makes us an instrument of injustice toward another, then we must be the counter-friction. In other words, we must say "no" and say "yes"—what we refuse to do and what we are willing to do are both expressions of the active soul.

Civil disobedience, then, is one way to go. Espousing the right rhetoric is another. Simple living is still another. *Walden* is worth reading as guidance for living simply and sustainably, as well as not getting to the end of our lives and realizing we had not lived. It forces us to ask key questions: what does it mean to be a whole human being and what it does it mean to be free? As such, it provides a political critique of growing industrial and capitalist production and labor conditions, and thus larger systems and structures.

Introduction

If we had listened to Thoreau long ago, we would not be in our current predicament. We didn't listen, and so the list of global eco-social ills is long and disturbing, but so is the list of active souls disturbing status quo habits and systems. Paul Hawken estimates there is more than two million groups worldwide working on eco-social change.[73] He is also the primary author of the Project Drawdown and Project Regeneration books and websites, which are filled with ideas and practices for a full response to climate crisis and injustice.

Thoreau wrote that "The highest we can attain to is not Knowledge but Sympathy with Intelligence."[74] Sympathy was likely Thoreau's favorite word, just like ecstasy was for Emerson. If we combine the sentiments from these beautifully suggestive words, we get this from Emerson in "Self-Reliance": "We lie in the lap of immense intelligence, which makes us receivers of its truth and organs of its activity. When we discern justice, when we discern truth, we do nothing of ourselves but allow a passage to its beams. If we ask whence this comes, if we seek to pry into the soul that causes, all philosophy is at fault. Its presence or its absence is all we can affirm."[75]

For both men, slavery was an affront to the presence of soul, and thus it was an affront to our collective and individual intelligence. The same was true for the wanton destruction of nature as techno-industrial-capitalist structures took hold. For the transcendentalists, self-culture, or transforming ourselves, was the first response, and that required the inner listening practice of self-reliance. The "inmost in due time becomes the outmost," Emerson wrote.[76] But the time is due; or rather, we are running out of time to do right by ourselves and the earth. The good news: When we get involved we are pushed to do self-work, and when we do self-work we are pushed to get involved. That is why Emerson and Thoreau called for political activism rooted in self-reliance and conscience and King included self-purification in his stages of resistance.

For Emerson, self-reliance is a condition for engaged citizenship and true democracy, and the more true democracy flourishes, the more we create the conditions for self-reliance. And by true, of course, I mean democracy grounded in Over-Soul, or the groundless ground expressed as the ongoing play of principles that inform ethical actions. Or, put more simply, love in action is the way to go. This high bar should not deter us; the real deterrence is not having guidance in an increasingly post-truth world.

And so, despite being imperfect humans and relatively slow joiners, when Emerson and Thoreau did join the abolitionist fight, they delivered some of the most significant and lasting attacks on the soulless institution of slavery while promoting the active soul. This volume provides six essays or speeches over nearly twenty years, three from each, that illustrate their stalwart adherence to higher law.

Emerson and Thoreau wrote many other essays and made other speeches attacking status quo institutions and calling for active resistance. Emerson's 1837 "The American Scholar" and 1838 "Divinity School Address," for example, called for the reform of education and religion, and Thoreau's "Life Without Principle" (published in 1863 but given in differing versions as a speech for many years prior) spoke out against the destructive materialism of gold rush times. Emerson's lengthy and influential 1836 "Nature," a largely spiritual essay, also questioned the politics of treating nature solely as commodity, while Thoreau's "Walking" states that "A town is saved…not more by the righteous men in it than by the woods and swamps that surround it."[77] To Thoreau, true reformers, and thus the truly righteous, are formed by contact with wildness.

The higher law ethos can be, and must be, applied to everything: to every injustice, to every cause, to every movement. But, again, the focus here is Emerson and Thoreau's soulful anti-slavery work. These six essays or speeches are core to their thought and their passion to turn ideas into action.

We need all the insights and wisdom we can muster. Emerson and Thoreau asked the right questions—the same questions we must ask—and provide inspiring examples of fitting responses to crisis. They were different in temperament yet joined in their pursuit of eco-social justice. We would be wise to follow their call to responsibility informed by debates over reform and civil disobedience.

NOTES

[1] Andrew Boyd. *I Want a Better Catastrophe: Navigating the Climate Crisis with Grief, Hope, and Gallows Humor* (BC, Canada: New Society Publishers, 2023).

[2] Emerson's views on the mechanization of humanity can be found in Barry Andrews's *American Sage: The Spiritual Teachings of Ralph Waldo Emerson* (Amherst: The University of Massachusetts Press, 2021), p. 167. See also his essay "Work and Days." Thoreau's questioning of whether railroads ride on us is from *Walden*. See *The Portable Thoreau*, edited by Carl Bode (New York: Penguin Books, 1975), 345.

[3] Laura Dassow Walls. *Henry David Thoreau: A Life* (Chicago: The University of Chicago Press, 2017), 288.

[4] Henry David Thoreau. *The Portable Thoreau*, edited by Carl Bode (New York: Penguin Books, 1975), 306.

[5] Hop Hopkins. "Racism is Killing the Planet," *Sierra: The Magazine of the Sierra Club*, June 8, 2020.

[6] Lawrence Buell, editor. *The American Transcendentalists: Essential Writings* (New York: Modern Library, 2006), xi, xxvii.

[7] Lawrence Buell. *Henry David Thoreau: Thinking Disobediently* (Oxford: Oxford University Press, 2023), 36, 37.

[8] Ralph Waldo Emerson. *The Portable Emerson*, edited by Carl Bode & Malcolm Cowley. (New York: Penguin Books, 1981), 224.

[9] Ibid., 212.

[10] Levine, Alan M. and Daniel S. Malachuk, editors. *A Political Companion to Ralph Waldo Emerson* (Lexington: The University Press of Kentucky, 2011), 2.

[11] Ralph Waldo Emerson. *The Political Emerson*, edited by David M. Robinson (Boston: Beacon Press, 2004), 46.

[12] Ibid., 35.

[13] Levine, Alan M. and Daniel S. Malachuk, editors. *A Political Companion to Ralph Waldo Emerson* (Lexington: The University Press of Kentucky, 2011), 5.

[14] Ibid., 7.

[15] Ralph Waldo Emerson. *The Political Emerson*, edited by David M. Robinson (Boston: Beacon Press, 2004), 77.

[16] Ralph Waldo Emerson. *Emerson's Antislavery Writings*, edited by Len Gougeon and Joel Myerson (New Haven: Yale University Press, 1995), xxii–xxiii.

[17] Ralph Waldo Emerson. *The Political Emerson*, edited by David M. Robinson (Boston: Beacon Press, 2004), 77.

[18] Levine, Alan M. and Daniel S. Malachuk, editors. *A Political Companion to Ralph Waldo Emerson* (Lexington: The University Press of Kentucky, 2011), 10.

[19] Ralph Waldo Emerson. *The Essential Writings of Ralph Waldo Emerson* (New York: Random House Modern Library Classics, 2000), 787.

[20] Ralph Waldo Emerson. *Emerson's Antislavery Writings*, edited by Len Gougeon and Joel Myerson (New Haven: Yale University Press, 1995), xi–lvi.

[21] Lawrence Buell. *Henry David Thoreau: Thinking Disobediently* (Oxford: Oxford University Press, 2023), 44–45.

[22] Ibid., 46.

[23] Laura Dassow Walls. *Henry David Thoreau: A Life* (Chicago, IL: The University of Chicago Press, 2017), 168.

[24] Material on Thoreau giving Emerson his own ethics can be found in the chapter on Thoreau in Robert D. Richardson Jr.'s *Emerson: The Mind on Fire* (Berkeley: University of California Press, 1995), 280–285.

[25] Lawrence Buell. *Henry David Thoreau: Thinking Disobediently* (Oxford, UK: Oxford University Press, 2023), 87.

Introduction

[26] Ibid., 91–93.

[27] Thoreau's "Slavery in Massachusetts" speech in response to the jailing of Anthony Burns is detailed in Laura Dassow Walls' *Henry David Thoreau: A Life* (Chicago: The University of Chicago Press, 2017), 345–347.

[28] Ralph Waldo Emerson. *Emerson's Antislavery Writings*, edited by Len Gougeon and Joel Myerson (New Haven: Yale University Press, 1995), xlv.

[29] Laura Dassow Walls. *Henry David Thoreau: A Life* (Chicago: The University of Chicago Press, 2017), 345–347.

[30] Walter Harding. *The Days of Henry Thoreau: A Biography* (Princeton: Princeton University Press, 1962), 418.

[31] Reynold, David S. "Transcendentalism, Transnationalism, and Antislavery Violence: Concord's Embrace of John Brown." In *Emerson for the 21st Century*, edited by Barry Tharaud. (Delaware: University of Delaware Press, 2010), 468.

[32] Ibid.

[33] Laura Dassow Walls. *Henry David Thoreau: A Life* (Chicago: The University of Chicago Press, 2017), 451–452.

[34] Ibid., 452.

[35] Ibid., 454–455.

[36] The Thoreau quotation, "I do not complain of any tactics that are effective of good, whether one wields the quill or the sword," is from a October 21, 1859 journal entry and can be found online at waldenwoods.org.

[37] Ibid., 451.

[38] James Marcus. *Glad to the Brink of Fear: A Portrait of Ralph Waldo Emerson* (Princeton, NJ: Princeton University Press, 2024), 221.

[39] Lawrence Buell, editor. *The American Transcendentalists: Essential Writings* (New York: Modern Library, 2006), 377.

[40] James Marcus. *Glad to the Brink of Fear: A Portrait of Ralph Waldo Emerson* (Princeton, NJ: Princeton University Press, 2024), 222.

[41] Peter Wirzbicki. *Fighting for the Higher Law: Black and White Transcendentalists Against Slavery* (Philadelphia: University of Pennsylvania Press, 2021), 3.

[42] Olivia B. Waxman, "What to the Slave is the Fourth of July? The History of Frederick Douglass' Searing Independence Day Oration," *Time Magazine*, June 26, 2020, time.com.

[43] Wen Stephenson. *What We're Fighting for Now is Each Other: Dispatches from the Front Lines of Climate Justice* (Boston, MA: Beacon Press, 2015), 24.

[44] Peter Wirzbicki. *Fighting for the Higher Law: Black and White Transcendentalists Against Slavery* (Philadelphia: University of Pennsylvania Press, 2021), 1–4.

[45] Ibid., 174.

[46] Ibid., 19–21.

[47] Ibid., 142–143.

[48] Lawrence Buell. *Henry David Thoreau: Thinking Disobediently* (Oxford: Oxford University Press, 2023), 89.

[49] Laura Dassow Walls. *Henry David Thoreau: A Life* (Chicago: The University of Chicago Press, 2017), 176.

[50] Ralph Waldo Emerson. *Emerson's Antislavery Writings*, edited by Len Gougeon and Joel Myerson (New Haven: Yale University Press, 1995), xxix–xxx.

[51] John J. Kucich. "Thoreau's Indian Problem: Savagism, Indigeneity, and the Politics of Place." In *Thoreau in an Age of Crisis: Uses and Abuses of an American Icon*, edited by Kristen Case, Rochelle Johnson, and Henrik Otterberg. (Paderborn, Germany: Brill-Fink, 2021).

Introduction

[52] Alda Balthrop-Lewis. *Thoreau's Religion: Walden Woods, Social Justice, and the Politics of Asceticism* (Cambridge, UK: Cambridge University Press, 2021), 9–13.

[53] Lawrence Buell. *Henry David Thoreau: Thinking Disobediently* (Oxford, UK: Oxford University Press, 2023), 24.

[54] The Thoreau quotation referencing Jesus is from an April 9, 1851 journal entry and can be found online at waldenwoods.org.

[55] Laura Dassow Walls. *Henry David Thoreau: A Life* (Chicago: The University of Chicago Press, 2017), 316–317.

[56] Levine, Alan M. and Daniel S. Malachuk, editors. *A Political Companion to Ralph Waldo Emerson* (Lexington: The University Press of Kentucky, 2011), 10–15.

[57] Lawrence Buell. *Henry David Thoreau: Thinking Disobediently* (Oxford: Oxford University Press, 2023), 87–99.

[58] Ibid., 38.

[59] James Marcus. *Glad to the Brink of Fear: A Portrait of Ralph Waldo Emerson* (Princeton, NJ: Princeton University Press, 2024), 226, 235.

[60] Martin Luther King, Jr's "Letter from a Birmingham Jail" can be found at www.letterfromjail.com, among numerous other online sources.

[61] Wen Stephenson. *What We're Fighting for Now is Each Other: Dispatches from the Front Lines of Climate Justice* (Boston: Beacon Press, 2015), 30–31.

[62] Erica Chenoweth. *Civil Resistance: What Everyone Needs to Know* (London: Oxford University Press, 2021).

[63] Andreas Malm. *How to Blow Up a Pipeline* (Brooklyn, New York: Verso Books, 2021), 56–57.

[64] Ibid., 41–42.

[65] Ibid., 46–49.

[66] Ibid., 54.

[67] Michael Schmitz. "Trump Embraces Lawlessness, but in the Name of a Higher Law." *The New York Times*, May 2, 2024.

[68] A transcript of Greta Thunberg's 2019 UN speech can be found at NPR.org.

[69] Martin Buber. *I and Thou*. Edited by Walter Kaufmann (New York: Scribner's, 1970).

[70] Henry David Thoreau. *The Portable Thoreau*, edited by Carl Bode (New York: Penguin Books, 1975), 263, 554.

[71] The Extinction Rebellion "We Quit" announcement can be found at www.extinctionrebellion.uk.

[72] Emerson's advice, "Let me never fall into the vulgar mistake of dreaming that I am persecuted whenever I am contradicted," is from a November 8, 1838 journal entry and can be found online.

[73] Paul Hawken. *Blessed Unrest: How the Largest Social Movement in History is Restoring Grace, Justice, and Beauty to the World* (New York: Penguin Books, 2008).

[74] Ralph Waldo Emerson and Henry David Thoreau. *Nature/Walking*, edited by John Elder (London: Oxford University Press, 2021), 113.

[75] Ralph Waldo Emerson. *The Portable Emerson*, edited by Carl Bode & Malcolm Cowley. (New York: Penguin Books, 1981), 150.

[76] Ibid., 138.

[77] Ralph Waldo Emerson and Henry David Thoreau. *Nature/Walking*, edited by John Elder (London: Oxford University Press, 2021), 100.

EMERSON, "THE OVER-SOUL"(1841)

Emerson opens "The Over-Soul" with this claim: "Our faith comes in moments; our vice is habitual." That might not sound like a stirring call to be active souls, and yet moments of faith rooted in spiritual experiences of the Over-Soul, or the higher law of unity-in-diversity, are transformative. They stay with us as we navigate a fragmented world of habitual vices instilled and perpetuated by societal institutions.

Emerson addresses the need to reform societal institutions in his 1841 essay "Man the Reformer," where he argues that "every man should be open to ecstasy or a divine illumination" and address their call to "cast aside all evil customs, timidities, and limitations, and be in his place a free and helpful man, a reformer...." Given his times, Emerson used "man" to mean humans generally; but not just any kind of human, a spiritually-informed and responsive human who does their great work in the world.

Emerson also addresses the need to reform societal institutions in his 1844 essay "New England Reformers," where he lists numerous reform movements, and applauds them, while also questioning their motives and methods when not connected to Over-Soul: "Every project in the history of reform, no matter how violent and surprising, is good, when it is the dictate of a man's genius and constitution, but very dull and suspicious when adopted from another." Emerson mentions an early and unexpected willingness to embrace violence here, but he only does so from the perspective of higher communications.

In his earlier 1837 speech "The American Scholar" he calls for the reform of education, and he does so forcefully, arguing that the "ancient precept" to know thyself and the "modern precept" to study nature must be integrated. Not surprisingly, the fount of that integration is the Soul of our soul, and thus "character is higher than intellect." And in his 1838 "Divinity School Address," he calls for the reform of religion, again with a focus on soul and character: "Truly speaking, it is not instruction, but provocation, that I can receive from another soul. What he announces, I must find true in me, or reject; and on his word, or as his second, be he who he may, I can accept nothing."

For Emerson, the Over-Soul inspires reform and then provides guidance once we begin the process of reform or instigate a reform movement. Moments of the right kind of faith, then, may be the wellspring of genuine spiritual and material progress. The power of our vices would seem to be without measure, but the reverberating power of the Over-Soul is by definition without measure.

Emerson argues that we must obey the dictates of the Over-Soul, which, especially to modern readers, may sound off-putting. "Obey" does not sound like it will lead to freedom. But to obey Over-Soul is to listen to and be guided by the deepest part of ourselves and fulfill our highest potential. To obey, in this good sense, increases freedom and lessens the influence of vices. But, as Emerson also argues, this takes wise discernment; if we are to be self-reliant our responses must be continually reconsidered and lived.

SOURCES

Emerson, Ralph Waldo. *The Portable Emerson*. Edited by Carl Bode & Malcolm Cowley. New York: Penguin Books, 1981.

Emerson, Ralph Waldo. *The Political Emerson*. Edited by David M. Robinson. Boston: Beacon Press, 2004.

THE OVER-SOUL

Ralph Waldo Emerson

But souls that of his own good life partake,
He loves as his own self; dear as his eye
They are to Him: He'll never them forsake:
When they shall die, then God himself shall die:
They live, they live in blest eternity.
—Henry More

Space is ample, east and west,
But two cannot go abreast,
Cannot travel in it two:
Yonder masterful cuckoo
Crowds every egg out of the nest,
Quick or dead, except its own;
A spell is laid on sod and stone,
Night and Day 've been tampered with,
Every quality and pith
Surcharged and sultry with a power
That works its will on age and hour.

There is a difference between one and another hour of life, in their authority and subsequent effect. Our faith comes in moments; our vice is habitual. Yet there is a depth in those brief moments which constrains us to ascribe more reality to them than to all other experiences. For this reason, the argument which is always forthcoming to silence those who conceive extraordinary hopes of man, namely, the appeal to experience, is for ever invalid and vain. We give up the past to the objector, and yet we hope. He must explain this hope.

We grant that human life is mean; but how did we find out that it was mean? What is the ground of this uneasiness of ours; of this old discontent? What is the universal sense of want and ignorance, but the fine inuendo by which the soul makes its enormous claim? Why do men feel that the natural history of man has never been written, but he is always leaving behind what you have said of him, and it becomes old, and books of metaphysics worthless? The philosophy of six thousand years has not searched the chambers and magazines of the soul. In its experiments there has always remained, in the last analysis, a residuum it could not resolve. Man is a stream whose source is hidden. Our being is descending into us from we know not whence. The most exact calculator has no prescience that somewhat incalculable may not balk the very next moment. I am constrained every moment to acknowledge a higher origin for events than the will I call mine.

As with events, so is it with thoughts. When I watch that flowing river, which, out of regions I see not, pours for a season its streams into me, I see that I am a pensioner; not a cause, but a surprised spectator of this ethereal water; that I desire and look up, and put myself in the attitude of reception, but from some alien energy the visions come.

The Supreme Critic on the errors of the past and the present, and the only prophet of that which must be, is that great nature in which we rest, as the earth lies in the soft arms of the atmosphere; that Unity, that Over-soul, within which every man's particular being is contained and made one with all other; that common heart, of which all sincere conversation is the worship, to which all right action is submission; that overpowering reality which confutes our tricks and talents, and constrains every one to pass for what he is, and to speak from his character, and not from his tongue, and which evermore tends to pass into our thought and hand, and become wisdom, and virtue, and power, and beauty. We live in succession, in division, in parts, in particles. Meantime within man is the soul of the whole; the wise silence; the universal beauty, to which every part and particle is equally related; the eternal ONE. And this deep power in which we exist, and whose beatitude is all accessible to us, is not only self-sufficing and perfect in every hour, but the act of seeing and the thing seen, the seer and the spectacle, the subject and the object, are one. We see the world piece by piece, as the sun, the moon, the animal, the tree; but the whole, of which these are the shining parts, is the soul. Only by the vision of that Wisdom can the horoscope of the ages be read, and by falling back on our better thoughts, by yielding to the spirit of prophecy which is innate in every man, we can know what it saith. Every man's words, who speaks from that life, must sound vain to those who do not dwell in the same thought on their own part. I dare not speak for it. My words do not carry its august sense; they fall short and cold. Only itself can inspire whom it will, and behold! their speech shall be lyrical, and sweet, and universal as the rising of the wind. Yet I desire, even by profane words, if I may not use sacred, to indicate the heaven of this deity, and to report what hints I have collected of the transcendent simplicity and energy of the Highest Law.

If we consider what happens in conversation, in reveries, in remorse, in times of passion, in surprises, in the instructions of dreams, wherein often we see ourselves in masquerade,—the droll disguises only magnifying and enhancing a real element, and forcing it on our distinct notice,—we shall catch many hints that will broaden and lighten into knowledge of the secret of nature. All goes to show that the soul in man is not an organ, but animates and exercises all the organs; is not a function, like the power of memory, of calculation, of comparison, but uses these as hands and feet; is not a faculty, but a light; is not the intellect or the will, but the master of the intellect and the will; is the background of our being, in which they lie,—an immensity not possessed and that cannot be possessed. From within or from behind, a light shines through us upon things, and makes us aware that we are nothing, but the light is all. A man is the facade of a temple wherein all wisdom and all good abide. What we commonly call man, the eating, drinking, planting, counting man, does not, as we know him, represent himself, but misrepresents himself. Him we do not respect, but the soul, whose organ he is, would he let it appear through his action, would make our knees bend. When it breathes through his intellect, it is genius; when it breathes through his will, it is virtue; when it flows through his affection, it is love. And the blindness of the intellect begins, when it would be something of itself. The weakness of the will begins, when the individual would be something of himself. All reform aims, in some one particular, to let the soul have its way through us; in other words, to engage us to obey.

Of this pure nature every man is at some time sensible. Language cannot paint it with his colors. It is too subtile. It is undefinable, unmeasurable, but we know that it pervades and contains us. We know that all spiritual being is in man. A wise old proverb says, "God comes to see us without bell"; that is, as there is no screen or ceiling between our heads and the infinite heavens, so is there no bar or wall in the soul where man, the effect, ceases, and God, the cause, begins. The walls are taken away. We lie open on one side to the deeps of spiritual nature, to the attributes of God. Justice we see and know, Love, Freedom, Power. These natures no man ever got above, but they tower over us, and most in the moment when our interests tempt us to wound them.

The sovereignty of this nature whereof we speak is made known by its independency of those limitations which circumscribe us on every hand. The soul circumscribes all things. As I have said, it contradicts all experience. In like manner it abolishes time and space. The influence of the senses has, in most men, overpowered the mind to that degree, that the walls of time and space have come to look real and insurmountable; and to speak with levity of these limits is, in the world, the sign of insanity. Yet time and space are but inverse measures of the force of the soul. The spirit sports with time,—

> "Can crowd eternity into an hour, Or stretch an hour to eternity."

We are often made to feel that there is another youth and age than that which is measured from the year of our natural birth. Some thoughts always find us young, and keep us so. Such a thought is the love of the universal and eternal beauty. Every man parts from that contemplation with the feeling that it rather belongs to ages than to mortal life. The least activity of the intellectual powers redeems us in a degree from the conditions of time. In sickness, in languor, give us a strain of poetry, or a profound sentence, and we are refreshed; or produce a volume of Plato, or Shakspeare, or remind us of their names, and instantly we come into a feeling of longevity. See how the deep, divine thought reduces centuries, and millenniums, and makes itself present through all ages. Is the teaching of Christ less effective now than it was when first his mouth was opened? The emphasis of facts and persons in my thought has nothing to do with time. And so, always, the soul's scale is one; the scale of the senses and the understanding is another. Before the revelations of the soul, Time, Space, and Nature shrink away. In common speech, we refer all things to time, as we habitually refer the immensely sundered stars to one concave sphere. And so we say that the Judgment is distant or near, that the Millennium approaches, that a day of certain political, moral, social reforms is at hand, and the like, when we mean, that, in the nature of things, one of the facts we contemplate is external and fugitive, and the other is permanent and connate with the soul. The things we now esteem fixed shall, one by one, detach themselves, like ripe fruit, from our experience, and fall. The wind shall blow them none knows whither. The landscape, the figures, Boston, London, are facts as fugitive as any institution past, or any whiff of mist or smoke, and so is society, and so is the world. The soul looketh steadily forwards, creating a world before her, leaving worlds behind her. She has no dates, nor rites, nor persons, nor specialties, nor men. The soul knows only the soul; the web of events is the flowing robe in which she is clothed.

After its own law and not by arithmetic is the rate of its progress to be computed. The soul's advances are not made by gradation, such as can be represented by motion in a straight line; but rather by ascension of state, such as can be represented by metamorphosis,—from the egg to the worm, from the worm to the fly. The growths of genius are of a certain *total* character, that does not advance the elect individual first over John, then Adam, then Richard, and give to each the pain of discovered inferiority, but by every throe of growth the man expands there where he works, passing, at each pulsation, classes, populations, of men. With each divine impulse the mind rends the thin rinds of the visible and finite, and comes out into eternity, and inspires and expires its air. It converses with truths that have always been spoken in the world, and becomes conscious of a closer sympathy with Zeno and Arrian, than with persons in the house.

This is the law of moral and of mental gain. The simple rise as by specific levity, not into a particular virtue, but into the region of all the virtues. They are in the spirit which contains them all. The soul requires purity, but purity is not it; requires justice, but justice is not that; requires beneficence, but is somewhat better; so that there is a kind of descent and accommodation felt when we leave speaking of moral nature, to urge a virtue which it enjoins. To the well-born child, all the virtues are natural, and not painfully acquired. Speak to his heart, and the man becomes suddenly virtuous.

Within the same sentiment is the germ of intellectual growth, which obeys the same law. Those who are capable of humility, of justice, of love, of aspiration, stand already on a platform that commands the sciences and arts, speech and poetry, action and grace. For whoso dwells in this moral beatitude already anticipates those special powers which men prize so highly. The lover has no talent, no skill, which passes for quite nothing with his enamoured maiden, however little she may possess of related faculty; and the heart which abandons itself to the Supreme Mind finds itself related to all its works, and will travel a royal road to particular knowledges and powers. In ascending to this primary and aboriginal sentiment, we have come from our remote station on the circumference instantaneously to the centre of the world, where, as in the closet of God, we see causes, and anticipate the universe, which is but a slow effect.

One mode of the divine teaching is the incarnation of the spirit in a form,—in forms, like my own. I live in society; with persons who answer to thoughts in my own mind, or express a certain obedience to the great instincts to which I live. I see its presence to them. I am certified of a common nature; and these other souls, these separated selves, draw me as nothing else can. They stir in me the new emotions we call passion; of love, hatred, fear, admiration, pity; thence comes conversation, competition, persuasion, cities, and war. Persons are supplementary to the primary teaching of the soul. In youth we are mad for persons. Childhood and youth see all the world in them. But the larger experience of man discovers the identical nature appearing through them all. Persons themselves acquaint us with the impersonal. In all conversation between two persons, tacit reference is made, as to a third party, to a common nature. That third party or common nature is not social; it is impersonal; is God. And so in groups where debate is earnest, and especially on high questions, the company become aware that the thought rises to an equal level in all bosoms, that all have a spiritual property in what was said, as well as the sayer. They all become wiser than they were. It arches over them like a temple, this unity of thought, in which every heart beats with nobler sense of power and duty, and thinks and acts with unusual solemnity. All are conscious of attaining to a higher self-possession. It shines for all. There is a certain wisdom of humanity which is common to the greatest men with the lowest, and which our ordinary education often labors to silence and obstruct. The mind is one, and the best minds, who love truth for its own sake, think much less of property in truth. They accept it thankfully everywhere, and do not label or stamp it with any man's name, for it is theirs long beforehand, and from eternity. The learned and the studious of thought have no monopoly of wisdom. Their violence of direction in some degree disqualifies them to think truly. We owe many valuable observations to people who are not very acute or profound, and who say the thing without effort, which we want and have long been hunting in vain. The action of the soul is oftener in that which is felt and left unsaid, than in that which is said in any conversation. It broods over every society, and they unconsciously seek for it in each other. We know better than we do. We do not yet possess ourselves, and we know at the same time that we are much more. I feel the same truth how often in my trivial conversation with my neighbours, that somewhat higher in each of us overlooks this by-play, and Jove nods to Jove from behind each of us.

Men descend to meet. In their habitual and mean service to the world, for which they forsake their native nobleness, they resemble those Arabian sheiks, who dwell in mean houses, and affect an external poverty, to escape the rapacity of the Pacha, and reserve all their display of wealth for their interior and guarded retirements.

As it is present in all persons, so it is in every period of life. It is adult already in the infant man. In my dealing with my child, my Latin and Greek, my accomplishments and my money stead me nothing; but as much soul as I have avails. If I am wilful, he sets his will against mine, one for one, and leaves me, if I please, the degradation of beating him by my superiority of strength. But if I renounce my will, and act for the soul, setting that up as umpire between us two, out of his young eyes looks the same soul; he reveres and loves with me.

The soul is the perceiver and revealer of truth. We know truth when we see it, let skeptic and scoffer say what they choose. Foolish people ask you, when you have spoken what they do not wish to hear, 'How do you know it is truth, and not an error of your own?' We know truth when we see it, from opinion, as we know when we are awake that we are awake. It was a grand sentence of Emanuel Swedenborg, which would alone indicate the greatness of that man's perception,—"It is no proof of a man's understanding to be able to confirm whatever he pleases; but to be able to discern that what is true is true, and that what is false is false, this is the mark and character of intelligence." In the book I read, the good thought returns to me, as every truth will, the image of the whole soul. To the bad thought which I find in it, the same soul becomes a discerning, separating sword, and lops it away. We are wiser than we know. If we will not interfere with our thought, but will act entirely, or see how the thing stands in God, we know the particular thing, and every thing, and every man. For the Maker of all things and all persons stands behind us, and casts his dread omniscience through us over things.

But beyond this recognition of its own in particular passages of the individual's experience, it also reveals truth. And here we should seek to reinforce ourselves by its very presence, and to speak with a worthier, loftier strain of that advent. For the soul's communication of truth is the highest event in nature, since it then does not give somewhat from itself, but it gives itself, or passes into and becomes that man whom it enlightens; or, in proportion to that truth he receives, it takes him to itself.

We distinguish the announcements of the soul, its manifestations of its own nature, by the term *Revelation*. These are always attended by the emotion of the sublime. For this communication is an influx of the Divine mind into our mind. It is an ebb of the individual rivulet before the flowing surges of the sea of life. Every distinct apprehension of this central commandment agitates men with awe and delight. A thrill passes through all men at the reception of new truth, or at the performance of a great action, which comes out of the heart of nature. In these communications, the power to see is not separated from the will to do, but the insight proceeds from obedience, and the obedience proceeds from a joyful perception. Every moment when the individual feels himself invaded by it is memorable. By the necessity of our constitution, a certain enthusiasm attends the individual's consciousness of that divine presence. The character and duration of this enthusiasm varies with the state of the individual, from an ecstasy and trance and prophetic inspiration,— which is its rarer appearance,—to the faintest glow of virtuous emotion, in which form it warms, like our household fires, all the families and associations of men, and makes society possible. A certain tendency to insanity has always attended the opening of the religious sense in men, as if they had been "blasted with excess of light." The trances of Socrates, the "union" of Plotinus, the vision of Porphyry, the conversion of Paul, the aurora of Behmen, the convulsions of George Fox and his Quakers, the illumination of Swedenborg, are of this kind. What was in the case of these remarkable persons a ravishment has, in innumerable instances in common life, been exhibited in less striking manner. Everywhere the history of religion betrays a tendency to enthusiasm. The rapture of the Moravian and Quietist; the opening of the internal sense of the Word, in the language of the New Jerusalem Church; the *revival* of the Calvinistic churches; the *experiences* of the Methodists, are varying forms of that shudder of awe and delight with which the individual soul always mingles with the universal soul.

The nature of these revelations is the same; they are perceptions of the absolute law. They are solutions of the soul's own questions. They do not answer the questions which the understanding asks. The soul answers never by words, but by the thing itself that is inquired after.

Revelation is the disclosure of the soul. The popular notion of a revelation is, that it is a telling of fortunes. In past oracles of the soul, the understanding seeks to find answers to sensual questions, and undertakes to tell from God how long men shall exist, what their hands shall do, and who shall be their company, adding names, and dates, and places. But we must pick no locks. We must check this low curiosity. An answer in words is delusive; it is really no answer to the questions you ask. Do not require a description of the countries towards which you sail. The description does not describe them to you, and to-morrow you arrive there, and know them by inhabiting them. Men ask concerning the immortality of the soul, the employments of heaven, the state of the sinner, and so forth. They even dream that Jesus has left replies to precisely these interrogatories. Never a moment did that sublime spirit speak in their *patois*. To truth, justice, love, the attributes of the soul, the idea of immutableness is essentially associated. Jesus, living in these moral sentiments, heedless of sensual fortunes, heeding only the manifestations of these, never made the separation of the idea of duration from the essence of these attributes, nor uttered a syllable concerning the duration of the soul. It was left to his disciples to sever duration from the moral elements, and to teach the immortality of the soul as a doctrine, and maintain it by evidences. The moment the doctrine of the immortality is separately taught, man is already fallen. In the flowing of love, in the adoration of humility, there is no question of continuance. No inspired man ever asks this question, or condescends to these evidences. For the soul is true to itself, and the man in whom it is shed abroad cannot wander from the present, which is infinite, to a future which would be finite.

These questions which we lust to ask about the future are a confession of sin. God has no answer for them. No answer in words can reply to a question of things. It is not in an arbitrary "decree of God," but in the nature of man, that a veil shuts down on the facts of to-morrow; for the soul will not have us read any other cipher than that of cause and effect. By this veil, which curtains events, it instructs the children of men to live in to-day. The only mode of obtaining an answer to these questions of the senses is to forego all low curiosity, and, accepting the tide of being which floats us into the secret of nature, work and live, work and live, and all unawares the advancing soul has built and forged for itself a new condition, and the question and the answer are one.

By the same fire, vital, consecrating, celestial, which burns until it shall dissolve all things into the waves and surges of an ocean of light, we see and know each other, and what spirit each is of. Who can tell the grounds of his knowledge of the character of the several individuals in his circle of friends? No man. Yet their acts and words do not disappoint him. In that man, though he knew no ill of him, he put no trust. In that other, though they had seldom met, authentic signs had yet passed, to signify that he might be trusted as one who had an interest in his own character. We know each other very well,—which of us has been just to himself, and whether that which we teach or behold is only an aspiration, or is our honest effort also.

We are all discerners of spirits. That diagnosis lies aloft in our life or unconscious power. The intercourse of society,—its trade, its religion, its friendships, its quarrels,— is one wide, judicial investigation of character. In full court, or in small committee, or confronted face to face, accuser and accused, men offer themselves to be judged. Against their will they exhibit those decisive trifles by which character is read. But who judges? and what? Not our understanding. We do not read them by learning or craft. No; the wisdom of the wise man consists herein, that he does not judge them; he lets them judge themselves, and merely reads and records their own verdict.

By virtue of this inevitable nature, private will is overpowered, and, maugre our efforts or our imperfections, your genius will speak from you, and mine from me. That which we are, we shall teach, not voluntarily, but involuntarily. Thoughts come into our minds by avenues which we never left open, and thoughts go out of our minds through avenues which we never voluntarily opened. Character teaches over our head. The infallible index of true progress is found in the tone the man takes. Neither his age, nor his breeding, nor company, nor books, nor actions, nor talents, nor all together, can hinder him from being deferential to a higher spirit than his own. If he have not found his home in God, his manners, his forms of speech, the turn of his sentences, the build, shall I say, of all his opinions, will involuntarily confess it, let him brave it out how he will. If he have found his centre, the Deity will shine through him, through all the disguises of ignorance, of ungenial temperament, of unfavorable circumstance. The tone of seeking is one, and the tone of having is another.

The great distinction between teachers sacred or literary,—between poets like Herbert, and poets like Pope,—between philosophers like Spinoza, Kant, and Coleridge, and philosophers like Locke, Paley, Mackintosh, and Stewart,—between men of the world, who are reckoned accomplished talkers, and here and there a fervent mystic, prophesying, half insane under the infinitude of his thought,—is, that one class speak *from within*, or from experience, as parties and possessors of the fact; and the other class, *from without*, as spectators merely, or perhaps as acquainted with the fact on the evidence of third persons. It is of no use to preach to me from without. I can do that too easily myself. Jesus speaks always from within, and in a degree that transcends all others. In that is the miracle. I believe beforehand that it ought so to be. All men stand continually in the expectation of the appearance of such a teacher. But if a man do not speak from within the veil, where the word is one with that it tells of, let him lowly confess it.

The same Omniscience flows into the intellect, and makes what we call genius. Much of the wisdom of the world is not wisdom, and the most illuminated class of men are no doubt superior to literary fame, and are not writers. Among the multitude of scholars and authors, we feel no hallowing presence; we are sensible of a knack and skill rather than of inspiration; they have a light, and know not whence it comes, and call it their own; their talent is some exaggerated faculty, some overgrown member, so that their strength is a disease. In these instances the intellectual gifts do not make the impression of virtue, but almost of vice; and we feel that a man's talents stand in the way of his advancement in truth. But genius is religious. It is a larger imbibing of the common heart. It is not anomalous, but more like, and not less like other men. There is, in all great poets, a wisdom of humanity which is superior to any talents they exercise. The author, the wit, the partisan, the fine gentleman, does not take place of the man. Humanity shines in Homer, in Chaucer, in Spenser, in Shakspeare, in Milton. They are content with truth. They use the positive degree. They seem frigid and phlegmatic to those who have been spiced with the frantic passion and violent coloring of inferior, but popular writers. For they are poets by the free course which they allow to the informing soul, which through their eyes beholds again, and blesses the things which it hath made. The soul is superior to its knowledge; wiser than any of its works. The great poet makes us feel our own wealth, and then we think less of his compositions. His best communication to our mind is to teach us to despise all he has done. Shakspeare carries us to such a lofty strain of intelligent activity, as to suggest a wealth which beggars his own; and we then feel that the splendid works which he has created, and which in other hours we extol as a sort of self-existent poetry, take no stronger hold of real nature than the shadow of a passing traveller on the rock. The inspiration which uttered itself in Hamlet and Lear could utter things as good from day to day, for ever. Why, then, should I make account of Hamlet and Lear, as if we had not the soul from which they fell as syllables from the tongue?

This energy does not descend into individual life on any other condition than entire possession. It comes to the lowly and simple; it comes to whomsoever will put off what is foreign and proud; it comes as insight; it comes as serenity and grandeur. When we see those whom it inhabits, we are apprized of new degrees of greatness. From that inspiration the man comes back with a changed tone. He does not talk with men with an eye to their opinion. He tries them. It requires of us to be plain and true. The vain traveller attempts to embellish his life by quoting my lord, and the prince, and the countess, who thus said or did to *him*. The ambitious vulgar show you their spoons, and brooches, and rings, and preserve their cards and compliments. The more cultivated, in their account of their own experience, cull out the pleasing, poetic circumstance,—the visit to Rome, the man of genius they saw, the brilliant friend they know; still further on, perhaps, the gorgeous landscape, the mountain lights, the mountain thoughts, they enjoyed yesterday,—and so seek to throw a romantic color over their life. But the soul that ascends to worship the great God is plain and true; has no rose-color, no fine friends, no chivalry, no adventures; does not want admiration; dwells in the hour that now is, in the earnest experience of the common day,—by reason of the present moment and the mere trifle having become porous to thought, and bibulous of the sea of light.

Converse with a mind that is grandly simple, and literature looks like word-catching. The simplest utterances are worthiest to be written, yet are they so cheap, and so things of course, that, in the infinite riches of the soul, it is like gathering a few pebbles off the ground, or bottling a little air in a phial, when the whole earth and the whole atmosphere are ours. Nothing can pass there, or make you one of the circle, but the casting aside your trappings, and dealing man to man in naked truth, plain confession, and omniscient affirmation.

Souls such as these treat you as gods would; walk as gods in the earth, accepting without any admiration your wit, your bounty, your virtue even,—say rather your act of duty, for your virtue they own as their proper blood, royal as themselves, and over-royal, and the father of the gods. But what rebuke their plain fraternal bearing casts on the mutual flattery with which authors solace each other and wound themselves! These flatter not. I do not wonder that these men go to see Cromwell, and Christina, and Charles the Second, and James the First, and the Grand Turk. For they are, in their own elevation, the fellows of kings, and must feel the servile tone of conversation in the world. They must always be a godsend to princes, for they confront them, a king to a king, without ducking or concession, and give a high nature the refreshment and satisfaction of resistance, of plain humanity, of even companionship, and of new ideas. They leave them wiser and superior men. Souls like these make us feel that sincerity is more excellent than flattery. Deal so plainly with man and woman, as to constrain the utmost sincerity, and destroy all hope of trifling with you. It is the highest compliment you can pay. Their "highest praising," said Milton, "is not flattery, and their plainest advice is a kind of praising."

Ineffable is the union of man and God in every act of the soul. The simplest person, who in his integrity worships God, becomes God; yet for ever and ever the influx of this better and universal self is new and unsearchable. It inspires awe and astonishment. How dear, how soothing to man, arises the idea of God, peopling the lonely place, effacing the scars of our mistakes and disappointments! When we have broken our god of tradition, and ceased from our god of rhetoric, then may God fire the heart with his presence. It is the doubling of the heart itself, nay, the infinite enlargement of the heart with a power of growth to a new infinity on every side. It inspires in man an infallible trust. He has not the conviction, but the sight, that the best is the true, and may in that thought easily dismiss all particular uncertainties and fears, and adjourn to the sure revelation of time, the solution of his private riddles. He is sure that his welfare is dear to the heart of being. In the presence of law to his mind, he is overflowed with a reliance so universal, that it sweeps away all cherished hopes and the most stable projects of mortal condition in its flood. He believes that he cannot escape from his good. The things that are really for thee gravitate to thee. You are running to seek your friend. Let your feet run, but your mind need not. If you do not find him, will you not acquiesce that it is best you should not find him? for there is a power, which, as it is in you, is in him also, and could therefore very well bring you together, if it were for the best. You are preparing with eagerness to go and render a service to which your talent and your taste invite you, the love of men and the hope of fame. Has it not occurred to you, that you have no right to go, unless you are equally willing to be prevented from going? O, believe, as thou livest, that every sound that is spoken over the round world, which thou oughtest to hear, will vibrate on thine ear! Every proverb, every book, every byword that belongs to thee for aid or comfort, shall surely come home through open or winding passages. Every friend whom not thy fantastic will, but the great and tender heart in thee craveth, shall lock thee in his embrace. And this, because the heart in thee is the heart of all; not a valve, not a wall, not an intersection is there anywhere in nature, but one blood rolls uninterruptedly an endless circulation through all men, as the water of the globe is all one sea, and, truly seen, its tide is one.

Let man, then, learn the revelation of all nature and all thought to his heart; this, namely; that the Highest dwells with him; that the sources of nature are in his own mind, if the sentiment of duty is there. But if he would know what the great God speaketh, he must 'go into his closet and shut the door,' as Jesus said. God will not make himself manifest to cowards. He must greatly listen to himself, withdrawing himself from all the accents of other men's devotion. Even their prayers are hurtful to him, until he have made his own. Our religion vulgarly stands on numbers of believers. Whenever the appeal is made—no matter how indirectly—to numbers, proclamation is then and there made, that religion is not. He that finds God a sweet, enveloping thought to him never counts his company. When I sit in that presence, who shall dare to come in? When I rest in perfect humility, when I burn with pure love, what can Calvin or Swedenborg say?

It makes no difference whether the appeal is to numbers or to one. The faith that stands on authority is not faith. The reliance on authority measures the decline of religion, the withdrawal of the soul. The position men have given to Jesus, now for many centuries of history, is a position of authority. It characterizes themselves. It cannot alter the eternal facts. Great is the soul, and plain. It is no flatterer, it is no follower; it never appeals from itself. It believes in itself. Before the immense possibilities of man, all mere experience, all past biography, however spotless and sainted, shrinks away. Before that heaven which our presentiments foreshow us, we cannot easily praise any form of life we have seen or read of. We not only affirm that we have few great men, but, absolutely speaking, that we have none; that we have no history, no record of any character or mode of living, that entirely contents us. The saints and demigods whom history worships we are constrained to accept with a grain of allowance. Though in our lonely hours we draw a new strength out of their memory, yet, pressed on our attention, as they are by the thoughtless and customary, they fatigue and invade. The soul gives itself, alone, original, and pure, to the Lonely, Original, and Pure, who, on that condition, gladly inhabits, leads, and speaks through it. Then is it glad, young, and nimble. It is not wise, but it sees through all things. It is not called religious, but it is innocent. It calls the light its own, and feels that the grass grows and the stone falls by a law inferior to, and dependent on, its nature. Behold, it saith, I am born into the great, the universal mind. I, the imperfect, adore my own Perfect. I am somehow receptive of the great soul, and thereby I do overlook the sun and the stars, and feel them to be the fair accidents and effects which change and pass. More and more the surges of everlasting nature enter into me, and I become public and human in my regards and actions. So come I to live in thoughts, and act with energies, which are immortal. Thus revering the soul, and learning, as the ancient said, that "its beauty is immense," man will come to see that the world is the perennial miracle which the soul worketh, and be less astonished at particular wonders; he will learn that there is no profane history; that all history is sacred; that the universe is represented in an atom, in a moment of time. He will weave no longer a spotted life of shreds and patches, but he will live with a divine unity. He will cease from what is base and frivolous in his life, and be content with all places and with any service he can render. He will calmly front the morrow in the negligency of that trust which carries God with it, and so hath already the whole future in the bottom of the heart.

THOREAU, "CIVIL DISOBEDIENCE" (1849)

"Civil Disobedience" was first published as "Resistance to Civil Government" and then quickly forgotten after receiving poor reviews. The catalyst for the essay was Thoreau's night in jail for refusing to pay a poll tax that supported slavery and the 1846–1848 war with Mexico over the annexation of Texas, which would increase the number of pro-slavery states, as well as the removal of Native Americans from their land. He was living at his Walden Pond cabin at the time, but he walked two miles to downtown Concord to pick up a repaired shoe. Sam Staples, the jailer, asked him to pay his tax and he again refused and then gladly went to jail.

Thoreau's friend and fellow transcendentalist, Bronson Alcott, was arrested three years prior for the same reason but he did not spend a night in jail. Alcott, not surprisingly, approved of his refusal; Emerson was not pleased, saying it was "mean and skulking, and in bad taste." He also questioned the logic of the protest, claiming that a state tax does not pay for the Mexican War, but buying taxed goods does. One would have to give up sugar, coats, books, etc. to be consistent. What Emerson missed is the symbolism. Thoreau turned the protest, which, we must admit, is minor in comparison to his defense of John Brown, into a seminal text filled with ideas on dissent.

The essay was republished in 1866 as "Civil Disobedience," and the arguments and phrase have resounded throughout the ages, including in the Civil Rights and climate justice movements. The core idea is the call to follow conscience, but that idea is enveloped in others: what it means to be a whole human being (like Emerson, he uses the gendered "man"), the need to disavow institutions and assay individual moral weaknesses that block that radical wholeness, and, ultimately, how to walk your talk.

An institutional and individual block is economic wealth. Thoreau makes it clear that most are willing to forgo conscience if it benefits them monetarily, even if the cost is losing our soul. This remains true, especially when 100 corporations produce more than 70 percent of greenhouse emissions and politicians are beholden to those corporations. For Thoreau, those who benefited from the economics of slavery are guilty of following expediency and the desire for order over instability. Today, those who benefit from the economics of fossil fuel extraction are guilty of expediency while defending business-as-usual. But slavery caused major instability and so does current climate injustice: as temperatures rise, both literally and metaphorically, so does the unequal distribution of its destruction.

Thoreau did not have much faith in democracy, which is too often influenced by political expediency, but he did not advocate for nonconformity for its own sake. He would be happy to conform to a just government and society. But when such justice is lacking, we must become a counter-friction, which might include direct action or withdrawing, in the sense of refusing to participate in the workings of injustice.

Thoreau opens "Civil Disobedience" by supporting the claim that least government is best, but he did so because the government of his time supported slavery. It does not follow that he would be for least government in our unstable climate crisis times when the diverse nature he loved dearly is increasingly being undermined by a lack of regulation on emissions. Thoreau's least government claim has been co-opted to support libertarianism, and his call for us to go in the "direction of our dreams" in *Walden* was once used in a Merrill Lynch commercial to sell its financial services, and by extension, the capitalist edifice he criticized. Thus, be warned when reading Thoreau's stirring words: one may mangle any text to fit a predetermined world view and "Civil Disobedience" may be especially ripe for misinterpretation.

Many factions and individuals across the globe have turned to "Civil Disobedience" to support their nonviolent causes (and violent ones). Often this turn is justified, but sometimes it isn't justified, and sometimes it may be hard to tell. For example, did government whistleblowers Julian Assange, Chelsea Manning, and Edward Snowden follow conscience? Were they heroes or traitors or are their cases more complex than that?

"Civil Disobedience" may be expressed by not paying a tax, withdrawing to a small cabin and discovering simple riches, and supporting and participating in direct action, like it did for Thoreau, or many other forms of resistance. The form is a matter of conscience, but appealing to individual conscience without connecting to collective Over-Soul and its many unfolding ethical principles must also be resisted.

SOURCES

Thoreau, Henry David. *The Portable Thoreau.* Edited by Carl Bode. New York: Penguin Books, 1975.

Walls, Laura Dassow. *Henry David Thoreau: A Life.* Chicago: The University of Chicago Press, 2017.

CIVIL DISOBEDIENCE

Henry David Thoreau

[1849, original title: Resistance to Civil Government]

I heartily accept the motto,—"That government is best which governs least;" and I should like to see it acted up to more rapidly and systematically. Carried out, it finally amounts to this, which also I believe—"That government is best which governs not at all;" and when men are prepared for it, that will be the kind of government which they will have. Government is at best but an expedient; but most governments are usually, and all governments are sometimes, inexpedient. The objections which have been brought against a standing army, and they are many and weighty, and deserve to prevail, may also at last be brought against a standing government. The standing army is only an arm of the standing government. The government itself, which is only the mode which the people have chosen to execute their will, is equally liable to be abused and perverted before the people can act through it. Witness the present Mexican war, the work of comparatively a few individuals using the standing government as their tool; for, in the outset, the people would not have consented to this measure.

This American government,—what is it but a tradition, though a recent one, endeavoring to transmit itself unimpaired to posterity, but each instant losing some of its integrity? It has not the vitality and force of a single living man; for a single man can bend it to his will. It is a sort of wooden gun to the people themselves; and, if ever they should use it in earnest as a real one against each other, it will surely split. But it is not the less necessary for this; for the people must have some complicated machinery or other, and hear its din, to satisfy that idea of government which they have. Governments show thus how successfully men can be imposed on, even impose on themselves, for their own advantage. It is excellent, we must all allow; yet this government never of itself furthered any enterprise, but by the alacrity with which it got out of its way. *It* does not keep the country free. *It* does not settle the West. *It* does not educate. The character inherent in the American people has done all that has been accomplished; and it would have done somewhat more, if the government had not sometimes got in its way. For government is an expedient, by which men would fain succeed in letting one another alone; and, as has been said, when it is most expedient, the governed are most let alone by it. Trade and commerce, if they were not made of India rubber, would never manage to bounce over obstacles which legislators are continually putting in their way; and, if one were to judge these men wholly by the effects of their actions, and not partly by their intentions, they would deserve to be classed and punished with those mischievous persons who put obstructions on the railroads.

But, to speak practically and as a citizen, unlike those who call themselves no-government men, I ask for, not at once no government, but *at once* a better government. Let every man make known what kind of government would command his respect, and that will be one step toward obtaining it.

After all, the practical reason why, when the power is once in the hands of the people, a majority are permitted, and for a long period continue, to rule, is not because they are most likely to be in the right, nor because this seems fairest to the minority, but because they are physically the strongest. But a government in which the majority rule in all cases can not be based on justice, even as far as men understand it. Can there not be a government in which the majorities do not virtually decide right and wrong, but conscience?—in which majorities decide only those questions to which the rule of expediency is applicable? Must the citizen ever for a moment, or in the least degree, resign his conscience to the legislator? Why has every man a conscience, then? I think that we should be men first, and subjects afterward. It is not desirable to cultivate a respect for the law, so much as for the right. The only obligation which I have a right to assume, is to do at any time what I think right. It is truly enough said that a corporation has no conscience; but a corporation of conscientious men is a corporation *with* a conscience. Law never made men a whit more just; and, by means of their respect for it, even the well-disposed are daily made the agents of injustice. A common and natural result of an undue respect for the law is, that you may see a file of soldiers, colonel, captain, corporal, privates, powder-monkeys and all, marching in admirable order over hill and dale to the wars, against their wills, aye, against their common sense and consciences, which makes it very steep marching indeed, and produces a palpitation of the heart. They have no doubt that it is a damnable business in which they are concerned; they are all peaceably inclined. Now, what are they? Men at all? or small movable forts and magazines, at the service of some unscrupulous man in power? Visit the Navy Yard, and behold a marine, such a man as an American government can make, or such as it can make a man with its black arts, a mere shadow and reminiscence of humanity, a man laid out alive and standing, and already, as one may say, buried under arms with funeral accompaniment, though it may be,—

> "Not a drum was heard, not a funeral note,
>   As his corpse to the ramparts we hurried;
> Not a soldier discharged his farewell shot
>   O'er the grave where our hero we buried."

The mass of men serve the State thus, not as men mainly, but as machines, with their bodies. They are the standing army, and the militia, jailers, constables, *posse comitatus*, &c. In most cases there is no free exercise whatever of the judgment or of the moral sense; but they put themselves on a level with wood and earth and stones; and wooden men can perhaps be manufactured that will serve the purpose as well. Such command no more respect than men of straw, or a lump of dirt. They have the same sort of worth only as horses and dogs. Yet such as these even are commonly esteemed good citizens. Others, as most legislators, politicians, lawyers, ministers, and office-holders, serve the state chiefly with their heads; and, as they rarely make any moral distinctions, they are as likely to serve the devil, without *intending* it, as God. A very few, as heroes, patriots, martyrs, reformers in the great sense, and *men*, serve the State with their consciences also, and so necessarily resist it for the most part; and they are commonly treated by it as enemies. A wise man will only be useful as a man, and will not submit to be "clay," and "stop a hole to keep the wind away," but leave that office to his dust at least:

> "I am too high-born to be propertied,
> To be a secondary at control,
> Or useful serving-man and instrument
> To any sovereign state throughout the world."

He who gives himself entirely to his fellow-men appears to them useless and selfish; but he who gives himself partially to them is pronounced a benefactor and philanthropist.

How does it become a man to behave toward the American government today? I answer that he cannot without disgrace be associated with it. I cannot for an instant recognize that political organization as *my* government which is the *slave's* government also.

All men recognize the right of revolution; that is, the right to refuse allegiance to and to resist the government, when its tyranny or its inefficiency are great and unendurable. But almost all say that such is not the case now. But such was the case, they think, in the Revolution of '75. If one were to tell me that this was a bad government because it taxed certain foreign commodities brought to its ports, it is most probable that I should not make an ado about it, for I can do without them: all machines have their friction; and possibly this does enough good to counter-balance the evil. At any rate, it is a great evil to make a stir about it. But when the friction comes to have its machine, and oppression and robbery are organized, I say, let us not have such a machine any longer. In other words, when a sixth of the population of a nation which has undertaken to be the refuge of liberty are slaves, and a whole country is unjustly overrun and conquered by a foreign army, and subjected to military law, I think that it is not too soon for honest men to rebel and revolutionize. What makes this duty the more urgent is that fact, that the country so overrun is not our own, but ours is the invading army.

Paley, a common authority with many on moral questions, in his chapter on the "Duty of Submission to Civil Government," resolves all civil obligation into expediency; and he proceeds to say, "that so long as the interest of the whole society requires it, that is, so long as the established government cannot be resisted or changed without public inconveniency, it is the will of God that the established government be obeyed, and no longer.... This principle being admitted, the justice of every particular case of resistance is reduced to a computation of the quantity of the danger and grievance on the one side, and of the probability and expense of redressing it on the other." Of this, he says, every man shall judge for himself. But Paley appears never to have contemplated those cases to which the rule of expediency does not apply, in which a people, as well as an individual, must do justice, cost what it may. If I have unjustly wrested a plank from a drowning man, I must restore it to him though I drown myself. This, according to Paley, would be inconvenient. But he that would save his life, in such a case, shall lose it. This people must cease to hold slaves, and to make war on Mexico, though it cost them their existence as a people.

In their practice, nations agree with Paley; but does anyone think that Massachusetts does exactly what is right at the present crisis?

"A drab of state, a cloth-o'-silver slut,
To have her train borne up, and her soul trail in the dirt."

Practically speaking, the opponents to a reform in Massachusetts are not a hundred thousand politicians at the South, but a hundred thousand merchants and farmers here, who are more interested in commerce and agriculture than they are in humanity, and are not prepared to do justice to the slave and to Mexico, *cost what it may*. I quarrel not with far-off foes, but with those who, near at home, co-operate with, and do the bidding of those far away, and without whom the latter would be harmless. We are accustomed to say, that the mass of men are unprepared; but improvement is slow, because the few are not materially wiser or better than the many. It is not so important that many should be as good as you, as that there be some absolute goodness somewhere; for that will leaven the whole lump. There are thousands who are *in opinion* opposed to slavery and to the war, who yet in effect do nothing to put an end to them; who, esteeming themselves children of Washington and Franklin, sit down with their hands in their pockets, and say that they know not what to do, and do nothing; who even postpone the question of freedom to the question of free-trade, and quietly read the prices-current along with the latest advices from Mexico, after dinner, and, it may be, fall asleep over them both. What is the price-current of an honest man and patriot today? They hesitate, and they regret, and sometimes they petition; but they do nothing in earnest and with effect. They will wait, well disposed, for others to remedy the evil, that they may no longer have it to regret. At most, they give only a cheap vote, and a feeble countenance and Godspeed, to the right, as it goes by them. There are nine hundred and ninety-nine patrons of virtue to one virtuous man; but it is easier to deal with the real possessor of a thing than with the temporary guardian of it.

All voting is a sort of gaming, like chequers or backgammon, with a slight moral tinge to it, a playing with right and wrong, with moral questions; and betting naturally accompanies it. The character of the voters is not staked. I cast my vote, perchance, as I think right; but I am not vitally concerned that that right should prevail. I am willing to leave it to the majority. Its obligation, therefore, never exceeds that of expediency. Even voting *for the right* is *doing* nothing for it. It is only expressing to men feebly your desire that it should prevail. A wise man will not leave the right to the mercy of chance, nor wish it to prevail through the power of the majority. There is but little virtue in the action of masses of men. When the majority shall at length vote for the abolition of slavery, it will be because they are indifferent to slavery, or because there is but little slavery left to be abolished by their vote. *They* will then be the only slaves. Only *his* vote can hasten the abolition of slavery who asserts his own freedom by his vote.

I hear of a convention to be held at Baltimore, or elsewhere, for the selection of a candidate for the Presidency, made up chiefly of editors, and men who are politicians by profession; but I think, what is it to any independent, intelligent, and respectable man what decision they may come to, shall we not have the advantage of his wisdom and honesty, nevertheless? Can we not count upon some independent votes? Are there not many individuals in the country who do not attend conventions? But no: I find that the respectable man, so called, has immediately drifted from his position, and despairs of his country, when his country has more reasons to despair of him. He forthwith adopts one of the candidates thus selected as the only *available* one, thus proving that he is himself *available* for any purposes of the demagogue. His vote is of no more worth than that of any unprincipled foreigner or hireling native, who may have been bought. Oh for a man who is a *man,* and, as my neighbor says, has a bone in his back which you cannot pass your hand through! Our statistics are at fault: the population has been returned too large. How many *men* are there to a square thousand miles in the country? Hardly one. Does not America offer any inducement for men to settle here? The American has dwindled into an Odd Fellow,—one who may be known by the development of his organ of gregariousness, and a manifest lack of intellect and cheerful self-reliance; whose first and chief concern, on coming into the world, is to see that the alms-houses are in good repair; and, before yet he has lawfully donned the virile garb, to collect a fund for the support of the widows and orphans that may be; who, in short, ventures to live only by the aid of the Mutual Insurance company, which has promised to bury him decently.

It is not a man's duty, as a matter of course, to devote himself to the eradication of any, even the most enormous wrong; he may still properly have other concerns to engage him; but it is his duty, at least, to wash his hands of it, and, if he gives it no thought longer, not to give it practically his support. If I devote myself to other pursuits and contemplations, I must first see, at least, that I do not pursue them sitting upon another man's shoulders. I must get off him first, that he may pursue his contemplations too. See what gross inconsistency is tolerated. I have heard some of my townsmen say, "I should like to have them order me out to help put down an insurrection of the slaves, or to march to Mexico,—see if I would go;" and yet these very men have each, directly by their allegiance, and so indirectly, at least, by their money, furnished a substitute. The soldier is applauded who refuses to serve in an unjust war by those who do not refuse to sustain the unjust government which makes the war; is applauded by those whose own act and authority he disregards and sets at naught; as if the State were penitent to that degree that it hired one to scourge it while it sinned, but not to that degree that it left off sinning for a moment. Thus, under the name of Order and Civil Government, we are all made at last to pay homage to and support our own meanness. After the first blush of sin, comes its indifference; and from immoral it becomes, as it were, *un*moral, and not quite unnecessary to that life which we have made.

The broadest and most prevalent error requires the most disinterested virtue to sustain it. The slight reproach to which the virtue of patriotism is commonly liable, the noble are most likely to incur. Those who, while they disapprove of the character and measures of a government, yield to it their allegiance and support, are undoubtedly its most conscientious supporters, and so frequently the most serious obstacles to reform. Some are petitioning the State to dissolve the Union, to disregard the requisitions of the President. Why do they not dissolve it themselves,—the union between themselves and the State,—and refuse to pay their quota into its treasury? Do not they stand in same relation to the State, that the State does to the Union? And have not the same reasons prevented the State from resisting the Union, which have prevented them from resisting the State?

How can a man be satisfied to entertain an opinion merely, and enjoy *it*? Is there any enjoyment in it, if his opinion is that he is aggrieved? If you are cheated out of a single dollar by your neighbor, you do not rest satisfied with knowing you are cheated, or with saying that you are cheated, or even with petitioning him to pay you your due; but you take effectual steps at once to obtain the full amount, and see that you are never cheated again. Action from principle, the perception and the performance of right, changes things and relations; it is essentially revolutionary, and does not consist wholly with anything which was. It not only divided states and churches, it divides families; aye, it divides the *individual*, separating the diabolical in him from the divine.

Unjust laws exist: shall we be content to obey them, or shall we endeavor to amend them, and obey them until we have succeeded, or shall we transgress them at once? Men generally, under such a government as this, think that they ought to wait until they have persuaded the majority to alter them. They think that, if they should resist, the remedy would be worse than the evil. But it is the fault of the government itself that the remedy *is* worse than the evil. *It* makes it worse. Why is it not more apt to anticipate and provide for reform? Why does it not cherish its wise minority? Why does it cry and resist before it is hurt? Why does it not encourage its citizens to be on the alert to point out its faults, and *do* better than it would have them? Why does it always crucify Christ, and excommunicate Copernicus and Luther, and pronounce Washington and Franklin rebels?

One would think, that a deliberate and practical denial of its authority was the only offence never contemplated by government; else, why has it not assigned its definite, its suitable and proportionate penalty? If a man who has no property refuses but once to earn nine shillings for the State, he is put in prison for a period unlimited by any law that I know, and determined only by the discretion of those who placed him there; but if he should steal ninety times nine shillings from the State, he is soon permitted to go at large again.

If the injustice is part of the necessary friction of the machine of government, let it go, let it go: perchance it will wear smooth,—certainly the machine will wear out. If the injustice has a spring, or a pulley, or a rope, or a crank, exclusively for itself, then perhaps you may consider whether the remedy will not be worse than the evil; but if it is of such a nature that it requires you to be the agent of injustice to another, then, I say, break the law. Let your life be a counter friction to stop the machine. What I have to do is to see, at any rate, that I do not lend myself to the wrong which I condemn.

As for adopting the ways which the State has provided for remedying the evil, I know not of such ways. They take too much time, and a man's life will be gone. I have other affairs to attend to. I came into this world, not chiefly to make this a good place to live in, but to live in it, be it good or bad. A man has not every thing to do, but something; and because he cannot do *every thing*, it is not necessary that he should do *something* wrong. It is not my business to be petitioning the Governor or the Legislature any more than it is theirs to petition me; and, if they should not hear my petition, what should I do then? But in this case the State has provided no way: its very Constitution is the evil. This may seem to be harsh and stubborn and unconcilliatory; but it is to treat with the utmost kindness and consideration the only spirit that can appreciate or deserves it. So is all change for the better, like birth and death which convulse the body.

I do not hesitate to say, that those who call themselves abolitionists should at once effectually withdraw their support, both in person and property, from the government of Massachusetts, and not wait till they constitute a majority of one, before they suffer the right to prevail through them. I think that it is enough if they have God on their side, without waiting for that other one. Moreover, any man more right than his neighbors constitutes a majority of one already.

I meet this American government, or its representative, the State government, directly, and face to face, once a year, no more, in the person of its tax-gatherer; this is the only mode in which a man situated as I am necessarily meets it; and it then says distinctly, Recognize me; and the simplest, the most effectual, and, in the present posture of affairs, the indispensablest mode of treating with it on this head, of expressing your little satisfaction with and love for it, is to deny it then. My civil neighbor, the tax-gatherer, is the very man I have to deal with,—for it is, after all, with men and not with parchment that I quarrel,—and he has voluntarily chosen to be an agent of the government. How shall he ever know well what he is and does as an officer of the government, or as a man, until he is obliged to consider whether he shall treat me, his neighbor, for whom he has respect, as a neighbor and well-disposed man, or as a maniac and disturber of the peace, and see if he can get over this obstruction to his neighborliness without a ruder and more impetuous thought or speech corresponding with his action? I know this well, that if one thousand, if one hundred, if ten men whom I could name,—if ten *honest* men only,—aye, if *one* HONEST man, in this State of Massachusetts, *ceasing to hold slaves*, were actually to withdraw from this copartnership, and be locked up in the county jail therefor, it would be the abolition of slavery in America. For it matters not how small the beginning may seem to be: what is once well done is done for ever. But we love better to talk about it: that we say is our mission. Reform keeps many scores of newspapers in its service, but not one man. If my esteemed neighbor, the State's ambassador, who will devote his days to the settlement of the question of human rights in the Council Chamber, instead of being threatened with the prisons of Carolina, were to sit down the prisoner of Massachusetts, that State which is so anxious to foist the sin of slavery upon her sister,—though at present she can discover only an act of inhospitality to be the ground of a quarrel with her,—the Legislature would not wholly waive the subject of the following winter.

Under a government which imprisons any unjustly, the true place for a just man is also a prison. The proper place today, the only place which Massachusetts has provided for her freer and less desponding spirits, is in her prisons, to be put out and locked out of the State by her own act, as they have already put themselves out by their principles. It is there that the fugitive slave, and the Mexican prisoner on parole, and the Indian come to plead the wrongs of his race, should find them; on that separate, but more free and honorable ground, where the State places those who are not *with* her but *against* her,—the only house in a slave-state in which a free man can abide with honor. If any think that their influence would be lost there, and their voices no longer afflict the ear of the State, that they would not be as an enemy within its walls, they do not know by how much truth is stronger than error, nor how much more eloquently and effectively he can combat injustice who has experienced a little in his own person. Cast your whole vote, not a strip of paper merely, but your whole influence. A minority is powerless while it conforms to the majority; it is not even a minority then; but it is irresistible when it clogs by its whole weight. If the alternative is to keep all just men in prison, or give up war and slavery, the State will not hesitate which to choose. If a thousand men were not to pay their tax-bills this year, that would not be a violent and bloody measure, as it would be to pay them, and enable the State to commit violence and shed innocent blood. This is, in fact, the definition of a peaceable revolution, if any such is possible. If the tax-gatherer, or any other public officer, asks me, as one has done, "But what shall I do?" my answer is, "If you really wish to do any thing, resign your office." When the subject has refused allegiance, and the officer has resigned his office, then the revolution is accomplished. But even suppose blood should flow. Is there not a sort of blood shed when the conscience is wounded? Through this wound a man's real manhood and immortality flow out, and he bleeds to an everlasting death. I see this blood flowing now.

I have contemplated the imprisonment of the offender, rather than the seizure of his goods,—though both will serve the same purpose,—because they who assert the purest right, and consequently are most dangerous to a corrupt State, commonly have not spent much time in accumulating property. To such the State renders comparatively small service, and a slight tax is wont to appear exorbitant, particularly if they are obliged to earn it by special labor with their hands. If there were one who lived wholly without the use of money, the State itself would hesitate to demand it of him. But the rich man—not to make any invidious comparison—is always sold to the institution which makes him rich. Absolutely speaking, the more money, the less virtue; for money comes between a man and his objects, and obtains them for him; it was certainly no great virtue to obtain it. It puts to rest many questions which he would otherwise be taxed to answer; while the only new question which it puts is the hard but superfluous one, how to spend it. Thus his moral ground is taken from under his feet. The opportunities of living are diminished in proportion as what are called the "means" are increased. The best thing a man can do for his culture when he is rich is to endeavor to carry out those schemes which he entertained when he was poor. Christ answered the Herodians according to their condition. "Show me the tribute-money," said he;—and one took a penny out of his pocket;—if you use money which has the image of Cæsar on it, and which he has made current and valuable, that is, *if you are men of the State*, and gladly enjoy the advantages of Cæsar's government, then pay him back some of his own when he demands it; "Render therefore to Cæsar that which is Cæsar's and to God those things which are God's,"—leaving them no wiser than before as to which was which; for they did not wish to know.

When I converse with the freest of my neighbors, I perceive that, whatever they may say about the magnitude and seriousness of the question, and their regard for the public tranquillity, the long and the short of the matter is, that they cannot spare the protection of the existing government, and they dread the consequences of disobedience to it to their property and families. For my own part, I should not like to think that I ever rely on the protection of the State. But, if I deny the authority of the State when it presents its tax-bill, it will soon take and waste all my property, and so harass me and my children without end. This is hard. This makes it impossible for a man to live honestly and at the same time comfortably in outward respects. It will not be worth the while to accumulate property; that would be sure to go again. You must hire or squat somewhere, and raise but a small crop, and eat that soon. You must live within yourself, and depend upon yourself, always tucked up and ready for a start, and not have many affairs. A man may grow rich in Turkey even, if he will be in all respects a good subject of the Turkish government. Confucius said: "If a State is governed by the principles of reason, poverty and misery are subjects of shame; if a State is not governed by the principles of reason, riches and honors are the subjects of shame." No: until I want the protection of Massachusetts to be extended to me in some distant southern port, where my liberty is endangered, or until I am bent solely on building up an estate at home by peaceful enterprise, I can afford to refuse allegiance to Massachusetts, and her right to my property and life. It costs me less in every sense to incur the penalty of disobedience to the State, than it would to obey. I should feel as if I were worth less in that case.

Some years ago, the State met me in behalf of the church, and commanded me to pay a certain sum toward the support of a clergyman whose preaching my father attended, but never I myself. "Pay it," it said, "or be locked up in the jail." I declined to pay. But, unfortunately, another man saw fit to pay it. I did not see why the schoolmaster should be taxed to support the priest, and not the priest the schoolmaster; for I was not the State's schoolmaster, but I supported myself by voluntary subscription. I did not see why the lyceum should not present its tax-bill, and have the State to back its demand, as well as the church. However, at the request of the selectmen, I condescended to make some such statement as this in writing:—"Know all men by these presents, that I, Henry Thoreau, do not wish to be regarded as a member of any incorporated society which I have not joined." This I gave to the town-clerk; and he has it. The State, having thus learned that I did not wish to be regarded as a member of that church, has never made a like demand on me since; though it said that it must adhere to its original presumption that time. If I had known how to name them, I should then have signed off in detail from all the societies which I never signed on to; but I did not know where to find such a complete list.

I have paid no poll-tax for six years. I was put into a jail once on this account, for one night; and, as I stood considering the walls of solid stone, two or three feet thick, the door of wood and iron, a foot thick, and the iron grating which strained the light, I could not help being struck with the foolishness of that institution which treated me as if I were mere flesh and blood and bones, to be locked up. I wondered that it should have concluded at length that this was the best use it could put me to, and had never thought to avail itself of my services in some way. I saw that, if there was a wall of stone between me and my townsmen, there was a still more difficult one to climb or break through, before they could get to be as free as I was. I did nor for a moment feel confined, and the walls seemed a great waste of stone and mortar. I felt as if I alone of all my townsmen had paid my tax. They plainly did not know how to treat me, but behaved like persons who are underbred. In every threat and in every compliment there was a blunder; for they thought that my chief desire was to stand the other side of that stone wall. I could not but smile to see how industriously they locked the door on my meditations, which followed them out again without let or hindrance, and *they* were really all that was dangerous. As they could not reach me, they had resolved to punish my body; just as boys, if they cannot come at some person against whom they have a spite, will abuse his dog. I saw that the State was half-witted, that it was timid as a lone woman with her silver spoons, and that it did not know its friends from its foes, and I lost all my remaining respect for it, and pitied it.

Thus the state never intentionally confronts a man's sense, intellectual or moral, but only his body, his senses. It is not armed with superior wit or honesty, but with superior physical strength. I was not born to be forced. I will breathe after my own fashion. Let us see who is the strongest. What force has a multitude? They only can force me who obey a higher law than I. They force me to become like themselves. I do not hear of *men* being *forced* to live this way or that by masses of men. What sort of life were that to live? When I meet a government which says to me, "Your money or your life," why should I be in haste to give it my money? It may be in a great strait, and not know what to do: I cannot help that. It must help itself; do as I do. It is not worth the while to snivel about it. I am not responsible for the successful working of the machinery of society. I am not the son of the engineer. I perceive that, when an acorn and a chestnut fall side by side, the one does not remain inert to make way for the other, but both obey their own laws, and spring and grow and flourish as best they can, till one, perchance, overshadows and destroys the other. If a plant cannot live according to its nature, it dies; and so a man.

The night in prison was novel and interesting enough. The prisoners in their shirt-sleeves were enjoying a chat and the evening air in the door-way, when I entered. But the jailer said, "Come, boys, it is time to lock up;" and so they dispersed, and I heard the sound of their steps returning into the hollow apartments. My room-mate was introduced to me by the jailer as "a first-rate fellow and a clever man." When the door was locked, he showed me where to hang my hat, and how he managed matters there. The rooms were whitewashed once a month; and this one, at least, was the whitest, most simply furnished, and probably the neatest apartment in town. He naturally wanted to know where I came from, and what brought me there; and, when I had told him, I asked him in my turn how he came there, presuming him to be an honest man, of course; and, as the world goes, I believe he was. "Why," said he, "they accuse me of burning a barn; but I never did it." As near as I could discover, he had probably gone to bed in a barn when drunk, and smoked his pipe there; and so a barn was burnt. He had the reputation of being a clever man, had been there some three months waiting for his trial to come on, and would have to wait as much longer; but he was quite domesticated and contented, since he got his board for nothing, and thought that he was well treated.

He occupied one window, and I the other; and I saw, that, if one stayed there long, his principal business would be to look out the window. I had soon read all the tracts that were left there, and examined where former prisoners had broken out, and where a grate had been sawed off, and heard the history of the various occupants of that room; for I found that even here there was a history and a gossip which never circulated beyond the walls of the jail. Probably this is the only house in the town where verses are composed, which are afterward printed in a circular form, but not published. I was shown quite a long list of verses which were composed by some young men who had been detected in an attempt to escape, who avenged themselves by singing them.

I pumped my fellow-prisoner as dry as I could, for fear I should never see him again; but at length he showed me which was my bed, and left me to blow out the lamp.

It was like travelling into a far country, such as I had never expected to behold, to lie there for one night. It seemed to me that I never had heard the town-clock strike before, nor the evening sounds of the village; for we slept with the windows open, which were inside the grating. It was to see my native village in the light of the Middle Ages, and our Concord was turned into a Rhine stream, and visions of knights and castles passed before me. They were the voices of old burghers that I heard in the streets. I was an involuntary spectator and auditor of whatever was done and said in the kitchen of the adjacent village inn—a wholly new and rare experience to me. It was a closer view of my native town. I was fairly inside of it. I never had seen its institutions before. This is one of its peculiar institutions; for it is a shire town. I began to comprehend what its inhabitants were about.

In the morning, our breakfasts were put through the hole in the door, in small oblong-square tin pans, made to fit, and holding a pint of chocolate, with brown bread, and an iron spoon. When they called for the vessels again, I was green enough to return what bread I had left; but my comrade seized it, and said that I should lay that up for lunch or dinner. Soon after, he was let out to work at haying in a neighboring field, whither he went every day, and would not be back till noon; so he bade me good-day, saying that he doubted if he should see me again.

When I came out of prison,—for some one interfered, and paid the tax,—I did not perceive that great changes had taken place on the common, such as he observed who went in a youth, and emerged a gray-headed man; and yet a change had to my eyes come over the scene,—the town, and State, and country,—greater than any that mere time could effect. I saw yet more distinctly the State in which I lived. I saw to what extent the people among whom I lived could be trusted as good neighbors and friends; that their friendship was for summer weather only; that they did not greatly purpose to do right; that they were a distinct race from me by their prejudices and superstitions, as the Chinamen and Malays are; that, in their sacrifices to humanity they ran no risks, not even to their property; that, after all, they were not so noble but they treated the thief as he had treated them, and hoped, by a certain outward observance and a few prayers, and by walking in a particular straight though useless path from time to time, to save their souls. This may be to judge my neighbors harshly; for I believe that most of them are not aware that they have such an institution as the jail in their village.

It was formerly the custom in our village, when a poor debtor came out of jail, for his acquaintances to salute him, looking through their fingers, which were crossed to represent the grating of a jail window, "How do ye do?" My neighbors did not thus salute me, but first looked at me, and then at one another, as if I had returned from a long journey. I was put into jail as I was going to the shoemaker's to get a shoe which was mended. When I was let out the next morning, I proceeded to finish my errand, and, having put on my mended shoe, joined a huckleberry party, who were impatient to put themselves under my conduct; and in half an hour,—for the horse was soon tackled,—was in the midst of a huckleberry field, on one of our highest hills, two miles off; and then the State was nowhere to be seen.

This is the whole history of "My Prisons."

I have never declined paying the highway tax, because I am as desirous of being a good neighbor as I am of being a bad subject; and, as for supporting schools, I am doing my part to educate my fellow-countrymen now. It is for no particular item in the tax-bill that I refuse to pay it. I simply wish to refuse allegiance to the State, to withdraw and stand aloof from it effectually. I do not care to trace the course of my dollar, if I could, till it buys a man, or a musket to shoot one with,—the dollar is innocent,—but I am concerned to trace the effects of my allegiance. In fact, I quietly declare war with the State, after my fashion, though I will still make use and get what advantages of her I can, as is usual in such cases.

If others pay the tax which is demanded of me, from a sympathy with the State, they do but what they have already done in their own case, or rather they abet injustice to a greater extent than the State requires. If they pay the tax from a mistaken interest in the individual taxed, to save his property or prevent his going to jail, it is because they have not considered wisely how far they let their private feelings interfere with the public good.

This, then, is my position at present. But one cannot be too much on his guard in such a case, lest his actions be biassed by obstinacy, or an undue regard for the opinions of men. Let him see that he does only what belongs to himself and to the hour.

I think sometimes, Why, this people mean well; they are only ignorant; they would do better if they knew how: why give your neighbors this pain to treat you as they are not inclined to? But I think, again, this is no reason why I should do as they do, or permit others to suffer much greater pain of a different kind. Again, I sometimes say to myself, When many millions of men, without heat, without ill-will, without personal feeling of any kind, demand of you a few shillings only, without the possibility, such is their constitution, of retracting or altering their present demand, and without the possibility, on your side, of appeal to any other millions, why expose yourself to this overwhelming brute force? You do not resist cold and hunger, the winds and the waves, thus obstinately; you quietly submit to a thousand similar necessities. You do not put your head into the fire. But just in proportion as I regard this as not wholly a brute force, but partly a human force, and consider that I have relations to those millions as to so many millions of men, and not of mere brute or inanimate things, I see that appeal is possible, first and instantaneously, from them to the Maker of them, and, secondly, from them to themselves. But, if I put my head deliberately into the fire, there is no appeal to fire or to the Maker of fire, and I have only myself to blame. If I could convince myself that I have any right to be satisfied with men as they are, and to treat them accordingly, and not according, in some respects, to my requisitions and expectations of what they and I ought to be, then, like a good Mussulman and fatalist, I should endeavor to be satisfied with things as they are, and say it is the will of God. And, above all, there is this difference between resisting this and a purely brute or natural force, that I can resist this with some effect; but I cannot expect, like Orpheus, to change the nature of the rocks and trees and beasts.

    I do not wish to quarrel with any man or nation. I do not wish to split hairs, to make fine distinctions, or set myself up as better than my neighbors. I seek rather, I may say, even an excuse for conforming to the laws of the land. I am but too ready to conform to them. Indeed I have reason to suspect myself on this head; and each year, as the tax-gatherer comes round, I find myself disposed to review the acts and position of the general and state governments, and the spirit of the people to discover a pretext for conformity.

> "We must affect our country as our parents,
> And if at any time we alienate
> Out love of industry from doing it honor,
> We must respect effects and teach the soul
> Matter of conscience and religion,
> And not desire of rule or benefit."

    I believe that the State will soon be able to take all my work of this sort out of my hands, and then I shall be no better patriot than my fellow-countrymen. Seen from a lower point of view, the Constitution, with all its faults, is very good; the law and the courts are very respectable; even this State and this American government are, in many respects, very admirable, and rare things, to be thankful for, such as a great many have described them; seen from a higher still, and the highest, who shall say what they are, or that they are worth looking at or thinking of at all?

However, the government does not concern me much, and I shall bestow the fewest possible thoughts on it. It is not many moments that I live under a government, even in this world. If a man is thought-free, fancy-free, imagination-free, that which *is not* never for a long time appearing *to be* to him, unwise rulers or reformers cannot fatally interrupt him.

I know that most men think differently from myself; but those whose lives are by profession devoted to the study of these or kindred subjects content me as little as any. Statesmen and legislators, standing so completely within the institution, never distinctly and nakedly behold it. They speak of moving society, but have no resting-place without it. They may be men of a certain experience and discrimination, and have no doubt invented ingenious and even useful systems, for which we sincerely thank them; but all their wit and usefulness lie within certain not very wide limits. They are wont to forget that the world is not governed by policy and expediency. Webster never goes behind government, and so cannot speak with authority about it. His words are wisdom to those legislators who contemplate no essential reform in the existing government; but for thinkers, and those who legislate for all time, he never once glances at the subject. I know of those whose serene and wise speculations on this theme would soon reveal the limits of his mind's range and hospitality. Yet, compared with the cheap professions of most reformers, and the still cheaper wisdom and eloquence of politicians in general, his are almost the only sensible and valuable words, and we thank Heaven for him. Comparatively, he is always strong, original, and, above all, practical. Still his quality is not wisdom, but prudence. The lawyer's truth is not Truth, but consistency or a consistent expediency. Truth is always in harmony with herself, and is not concerned chiefly to reveal the justice that may consist with wrong-doing. He well deserves to be called, as he has been called, the Defender of the Constitution. There are really no blows to be given by him but defensive ones. He is not a leader, but a follower. His leaders are the men of '87. "I have never made an effort," he says, "and never propose to make an effort; I have never countenanced an effort, and never mean to countenance an effort, to disturb the arrangement as originally made, by which the various States came into the Union." Still thinking of the sanction which the Constitution gives to slavery, he says, "Because it was part of the original compact,—let it stand." Notwithstanding his special acuteness and ability, he is unable to take a fact out of its merely political relations, and behold it as it lies absolutely to be disposed of by the intellect,—what, for instance, it behoves a man to do here in America today with regard to slavery, but ventures, or is driven, to make some such desperate answer as the following, while professing to speak absolutely, and as a private man,—from which what new and singular code of social duties might be inferred? "The manner," says he, "in which the governments of those States where slavery exists are to regulate it, is for their own consideration, under the responsibility to their constituents, to the general laws of propriety, humanity, and justice, and to God. Associations formed elsewhere, springing from a feeling of humanity, or any other cause, have nothing whatever to do with it. They have never received any encouragement from me and they never will."[*]

They who know of no purer sources of truth, who have traced up its stream no higher, stand, and wisely stand, by the Bible and the Constitution, and drink at it there with reverence and humanity; but they who behold where it comes trickling into this lake or that pool, gird up their loins once more, and continue their pilgrimage toward its fountain-head.

No man with a genius for legislation has appeared in America. They are rare in the history of the world. There are orators, politicians, and eloquent men, by the thousand; but the speaker has not yet opened his mouth to speak who is capable of settling the much-vexed questions of the day. We love eloquence for its own sake, and not for any truth which it may utter, or any heroism it may inspire. Our legislators have not yet learned the comparative value of free-trade and of freedom, of union, and of rectitude, to a nation. They have no genius or talent for comparatively humble questions of taxation and finance, commerce and manufactures and agriculture. If we were left solely to the wordy wit of legislators in Congress for our guidance, uncorrected by the seasonable experience and the effectual complaints of the people,

---

[*] These extracts have been inserted since the Lecture was read—HDT.

America would not long retain her rank among the nations. For eighteen hundred years, though perchance I have no right to say it, the New Testament has been written; yet where is the legislator who has wisdom and practical talent enough to avail himself of the light which it sheds on the science of legislation.

The authority of government, even such as I am willing to submit to,—for I will cheerfully obey those who know and can do better than I, and in many things even those who neither know nor can do so well,—is still an impure one: to be strictly just, it must have the sanction and consent of the governed. It can have no pure right over my person and property but what I concede to it. The progress from an absolute to a limited monarchy, from a limited monarchy to a democracy, is a progress toward a true respect for the individual. Even the Chinese philosopher was wise enough to regard the individual as the basis of the empire. Is a democracy, such as we know it, the last improvement possible in government? Is it not possible to take a step further towards recognizing and organizing the rights of man? There will never be a really free and enlightened State, until the State comes to recognize the individual as a higher and independent power, from which all its own power and authority are derived, and treats him accordingly. I please myself with imagining a State at last which can afford to be just to all men, and to treat the individual with respect as a neighbor; which even would not think it inconsistent with its own repose, if a few were to live aloof from it, not meddling with it, nor embraced by it, who fulfilled all the duties of neighbors and fellow-men. A State which bore this kind of fruit, and suffered it to drop off as fast as it ripened, would prepare the way for a still more perfect and glorious State, which also I have imagined, but not yet anywhere seen.

EMERSON, "THE FUGITIVE SLAVE LAW" (1854)

Emerson's first "The Fugitive Slave Law" speech in 1851 is his response to the law and its primary promoter, Daniel Webster. Webster, a Massachusetts senator, gave an infamous Seventh of March address to Congress, in which he put his substantial political weight behind poorly-enforced existing laws that deemed slaves as property that must be returned to their owners. The Fugitive Slave Law would enact his words, but the speech ruined his reputation in the North (it was enhanced in the South). He would lose his senate seat, although he became Secretary of State under Millard Fillmore before dying in 1852.

Webster had a long senate career and was well-regarded by Emerson; or rather, he was well-regarded until that address. When citizens in the North were forced to be accomplices to slavery, he fumed. He already knew the North was complicit, but the Act was unconscionable and took this complicity to another level, or a lower level that not only ignored higher law but willfully debased it.

Emerson was fond of what he called "representative men" who embodied self-reliance and ethical principles. He gave a series of lectures on various historical figures, including Plato, Montaigne, and Goethe, which would later become the book *Representative Men*. Emerson also honored and deeply valued women, such as his aunt, Mary Moody Emerson, and Margaret Fuller, who had great influence on his life. His regard for the self-reliant did not include hero worship, but was an invitation to learn virtues we may embody in our own lives. It is safe to say Daniel Webster failed the test. Thoreau references Webster in "Civil Disobedience" but mostly leaves him unnamed. Emerson not only names him but lets him have it. He argues that Webster, and others that support the Act, and the Act itself, reveal humanity at our treacherous worst.

His 1851 speech was an address to fellow citizens of Concord on May 3rd, and thus is another example of Emerson the public intellectual but also a respected and active soul member of the community. All institutions need reform, Emerson argued, but especially slavery, given that it is so heinous and so counter to higher law. Emerson biographer James Marcus called the address "a scorcher" and the "angriest, darkest, and most ferocious of his career." More scorchers would follow, including this 1854 "The Fugitive Slave Law" address to a large crowd in New York, in which he would continue to lambaste Webster on the fourth anniversary of his infamous support of slavery.

Marcus also points out that Emerson gave many more speeches and he was a consistent voice putting intense pressure on anti-abolitionists and the government. The slow-to-get involved Emerson gave his first antislavery address in 1837 and focused it on the importance of free speech to reform. He did so for good reason: Elijah P. Lovejoy, an abolitionist publisher, was killed in that year. Still, abolitionists did not think the address was fiery enough. He then took a big step in his 1844 British West Indies address on the anniversary of emancipation, where he countered the then-common claim of Black inferiority. His "The Fugitive Slave

Law" speeches signified another big step. Emerson was all-in, taking on Webster, or anyone or anything that was on the wrong side of abolitionism.

Thoreau was often more radical than Emerson, but in his "New England Reformers" lecture, given five months before his British West Indies address, he argued that our inner genius often makes us radical in politics: Men are "conservatives after dinner, or before taking their rest; when they are sick, or aged: in the morning, or when their intellect or their conscience has been aroused, when they hear music, or when they read poetry, they are radicals."

Emerson's radical responses would vacillate depending on the situation, but with each unfolding year, and each unfolding tragedy, his inner genius led him to focus less on Over-Soul as transcendental ideal and more on turning this ideal into action.

SOURCES

Emerson, Ralph Waldo. *The Portable Emerson*. Edited by Carl Bode & Malcolm Cowley. New York: Penguin Books, 1981.

Emerson, Ralph Waldo. *The Political Emerson*. Edited by David M. Robinson. Boston: Beacon Press, 2004.

Emerson, Ralph Waldo. *Emerson's Antislavery Writings*. Edited by Len Gougeon and Joel Myerson. New Haven: Yale University Press, 1995.

Marcus, James. *Glad to the Brink of Fear: A Portrait of Ralph Waldo Emerson*. Princeton: Princeton University Press, 2024.

THE FUGITIVE SLAVE LAW

Ralph Waldo Emerson

[THE FUGITIVE SLAVE LAW—Lecture at New York]

Lecture Read in the Tabernacle, New York City March 7, 1854, on the Fourth Anniversary of Daniel Webster's Speech in Favor of the Bill

"OF all we loved and honored, naught
Save power remains,—
A fallen angel's pride of thought,
Still strong in chains.
  All else is gone; from those great eyes
The soul has fled:
When faith is lost, when honor dies,
The man is dead!"
Whittier, Ichabod!

"WE that had loved him so, followed him, honoured him,
Lived in his mild and magnificent eye,
Learned his great language, caught his clear accents,
Made him our patter to live and to die!
Shakspeare was of us, Milton was for us,
Burns, Shelley, were with us,—they watch from their graves!
He alone breaks from the van and the freemen,

—He alone sinks to the rear and the slaves!"
Browning, "The Lost Leader"

I DO not often speak to public questions;—they are odious and hurtful, and it seems like meddling or leaving your work. I have my own spirits in prison;—spirits in deeper prisons, whom no man visits if I do not. And then I see what havoc it makes with any good mind, a dissipated philanthropy. The one thing not to be forgiven to intellectual persons is, not to know their own task, or to take their ideas from others. From this want of manly rest in their own and rash acceptance of other people's watchwords come the imbecility and fatigue of their conversation. For they cannot affirm these from any original experience, and of course not with the natural movement and total strength of their nature and talent, but only from their memory, only from their cramped position of standing for their teacher. They say what they would have you believe, but what they do not quite know.

My own habitual view is to the well-being of students or scholars. And it is only when the public event affects them, that it very seriously touches me. And what I have to say is to them. For every man speaks mainly to a class whom he works with and more or less fully represents. It is to these I am beforehand related and engaged, in this audience or out of it—to them and not to others. And yet, when I say the class of scholars or students,—that is a class which comprises in some sort all mankind, comprises every man in the best hours of his life; and in these days not only virtually but actually. For who are the readers and thinkers of 1854? Owing to the silent revolution which the newspaper has wrought, this class has come in this country to take in all classes. Look into the morning trains which, from every suburb, carry the business men into the city to their shops, counting-rooms, work-yards and warehouses. With them enters the car—the newsboy, that humble priest of politics, finance, philosophy, and religion. He unfolds his magical sheets,—twopence a head his bread of knowledge costs—and instantly the entire rectangular assembly, fresh from their breakfast, are bending as one man to their second breakfast. There is, no doubt, chaff enough in what he brings; but there is fact, thought, and wisdom in the crude mass, from all regions of the world.

I have lived all my life without suffering any known inconvenience from American Slavery. I never saw it; I never heard the whip; I never felt the check on my free speech and action, until, the other day, when Mr. Webster, by his personal influence, brought the Fugitive Slave Law on the country. I say Mr. Webster, for though the Bill was not his, it is yet notorious that he was the life and soul of it, that he gave it all he had: it cost him his life, and under the shadow of his great name inferior men sheltered themselves, threw their ballots for it and made the law. I say inferior men. There were all sorts of what are called brilliant men, accomplished men, men of high station, a President of the United States, Senators, men of eloquent speech, but men without self-respect, without character, and it was strange to see that office, age, fame, talent, even a repute for honesty, all count for nothing. They had no opinions, they had no memory for what they had been saying like the Lord's Prayer all their lifetime: they were only looking to what their great Captain did: if he jumped, they jumped, if he stood on his head, they did. In ordinary, the supposed sense of their district and State is their guide, and that holds them to the part of liberty and justice. But it is always a little difficult to decipher what this public sense is; and when a great man comes who knots up into himself the opinions and wishes of the people, it is so much easier to follow him as an exponent of this. He too is responsible; they will not be. It will always suffice to say,—"I followed him."

I saw plainly that the great show their legitimate power in nothing more than in their power to misguide us. I saw that a great man, deservedly admired for his powers and their general right direction, was able,—fault of the total want of stamina in public men,—when he failed, to break them all with him, to carry parties with him.

In what I have to say of Mr. Webster I do not confound him with vulgar politicians before or since. There is always base ambition enough, men who calculate on the immense ignorance of the masses; that is their quarry and farm: they use the constituencies at home only for their shoes. And, of course, they can drive out from the contest any honorable man. The low can best win the low, and all men like to be made much of. There are those too who have power and inspiration only to do ill. Their talent or their faculty deserts them when they undertake anything right. Mr. Webster had a natural ascendancy of aspect and carriage which distinguished him over all his contemporaries. His countenance, his figure, and his manners were all in so grand a style, that he was, without effort, as superior to his most eminent rivals as they were to the humblest; so that his arrival in any place was an event which drew crowds of people, who went to satisfy their eyes, and could not see him enough. I think they looked at him as the representative of the American Continent. He was there in his Adamitic capacity, as if he alone of all men did not disappoint the eye and the ear, but was a fit figure in the landscape.

I remember his appearance at Bunker's Hill. There was the Monument, and here was Webster. He knew well that a little more or less of rhetoric signified nothing: he was only to say plain and equal things,—grand things if he had them, and, if he had them not, only to abstain from saying unfit things,—and the whole occasion was answered by his presence. It was a place for behavior more than for speech, and Mr. Webster walked through his part with entire success. His excellent organization, the perfection of his elocution and all that thereto belongs,—voice, accent, intonation, attitude, manner,—we shall not soon find again. Then he was so thoroughly simple and wise in his rhetoric; he saw through his matter, hugged his fact so close, went to the principle or essential, and never indulged in a weak flourish, though he knew perfectly well how to make such exordiums, episodes and perorations as might give perspective to his harangues without in the least embarrassing his march or confounding his transitions. In his statement things lay in daylight; we saw them in order as they were. Though he knew very well how to present his own personal claims, yet in his argument he was intellectual,—stated his fact pure of all personality, so that his splendid wrath, when his eyes became lamps, was the wrath of the fact and the cause he stood for.

His power, like that of all great masters, was not in excellent parts, but was total. He had a great and everywhere equal propriety. He worked with that closeness of adhesion to the matter in hand which a joiner or a chemist uses, and the same quiet and sure feeling of right to his place that an oak or a mountain have to theirs. After all his talents have been described, there remains that perfect propriety which animated all the details of the action or speech with the character of the whole, so that his beauties of detail are endless. He seemed born for the bar, born for the senate, and took very naturally a leading part in large private and in public affairs; for his head distributed things in their right places, and what he saw so well he compelled other people to see also. Great is the privilege of eloquence. What gratitude does every man feel to him who speaks well for the right,—who translates truth into language entirely plain and clear!

The history of this country has given a disastrous importance to the defects of this great man's mind. Whether evil influences and the corruption of politics, or whether original infirmity, it was the misfortune of his country that with this large understanding he had not what is better than intellect, and the source of its health. It is a law of our nature that great thoughts come from the heart. If his moral sensibility had been proportioned to the force of his understanding, what limits could have been set to his genius and beneficent power? But he wanted that deep source of inspiration. Hence a sterility of thought, the want of generalization in his speeches, and the curious fact that, with a general ability which impresses all the world, there is not a single general remark, not an observation on life and manners, not an aphorism that can pass into literature from his writings.

Four years ago to-night, on one of those high critical moments in history when great issues are determined, when the powers of right and wrong are mustered for conflict, and it lies with one man to give a casting vote,—Mr. Webster, most unexpectedly, threw his whole weight on the side of

Slavery, and caused by his personal and official authority the passage of the Fugitive Slave Bill.

It is remarked of the Americans that they value dexterity too much, and honor too little; that they think they praise a man more by saying that he is "smart" than by saying that he is right. Whether the defect be national or not, it is the defect and calamity of Mr. Webster; and it is so far true of his countrymen, namely, that the appeal is sure to be made to his physical and mental ability when his character is assailed. His speeches on the seventh of March, and at Albany, at Buffalo, at Syracuse and Boston are cited in justification. And Mr. Webster's literary editor believes that it was his wish to rest his fame on the speech of the seventh of March. Now, though I have my own opinions on this seventh of March discourse and those others, and think them very transparent and very open to criticism,—yet the secondary merits of a speech, namely, its logic, its illustrations, its points, etc., are not here in question. Nobody doubts that Daniel Webster could make a good speech. Nobody doubts that there were good and plausible things to be said on the part of the South. But this is not a question of ingenuity, not a question of syllogisms, but of sides. *How came he there?*

There are always texts and thoughts and arguments. But it is the genius and temper of the man which decides whether he will stand for right or for might. Who doubts the power of any fluent debater to defend either of our political parties, or any client in our courts? There was the same law in England for Jeffries and Talbot and Yorke to read slavery out of, and for Lord Mansfield to read freedom. And in this country one sees that there is always margin enough in the statute for a liberal judge to read one way and a servile judge another.

But the question which History will ask is broader. In the final hour, when he was forced by the peremptory necessity of the closing armies to take a side,—did he take the part of great principles, the side of humanity and justice, or the side of abuse and oppression and chaos?

Mr. Webster decided for Slavery, and that, when the aspect of the institution was no longer doubtful, no longer feeble and apologetic and proposing soon to end itself, but when it was strong, aggressive, and threatening an illimitable increase. He listened to State reasons and hopes, and left, with much complacency we are told, the testament of his speech to the astonished State of Massachusetts, *vera pro gratis;* a ghastly result of all those years of experience in affairs, this, that there was nothing better for the foremost American man to tell his countrymen than that Slavery was now at that strength that they must beat down their conscience and become kidnappers for it.

This was like the doleful speech falsely ascribed to the patriot Brutus: "Virtue, I have followed thee through life, and I find thee but a shadow." Here was a question of an immoral law; a question agitated for ages, and settled always in the same way by every great jurist, that an immoral law cannot be valid. Cicero, Grotius, Coke, Blackstone, Burlamaqui, Vattel, Burke, Jefferson, do all affirm this, and I cite them, not that they can give evidence to what is indisputable, but because, though lawyers and practical statesmen, the habit of their profession did not hide from them that this truth was the foundation of States.

Here was the question, Are you for man and for the good of man; or are you for the hurt and harm of man? It was the question whether man shall be treated as leather?

whether the Negro shall be, as the Indians were in Spanish America, a piece of money? Whether this system, which is a kind of mill or factory for converting men into monkeys, shall be upheld and enlarged? And Mr. Webster and the country went for the application to these poor men of quadruped law.

People were expecting a totally different course from Mr. Webster. If any man had in that hour possessed the weight with the country which he had acquired, he could have brought the whole country to its senses. But not a moment's pause was allowed. Angry parties went from bad to worse, and the decision of Webster was accompanied with everything offensive to freedom and good morals. There was something like an attempt to debauch the moral sentiment of the clergy and of the youth. Burke said he "would pardon something to the spirit of liberty." But by Mr. Webster the opposition to the law was sharply called treason, and prosecuted so. He told the people at Boston "they must conquer their prejudices;" that "agitation of the subject of Slavery must be suppressed." He did as immoral men usually do, made very low bows to the Christian Church, and went through all the Sunday decorums; but when allusion was made to the question of duty and the sanctions of morality, he very frankly said, at Albany, "Some higher law, something existing somewhere between here and the third heaven,—I do not know where." And if the reporters say true, this wretched atheism found some laughter in the company.

I said I had never in my life up to this time suffered from the Slave Institution. Slavery in Virginia or Carolina was like Slavery in Africa or the Feejees, for me. There was an old fugitive law, but it had become, or was fast becoming, a dead letter, and, by the genius and laws of Massachusetts, inoperative. The new Bill made it operative, required me to hunt slaves, and it found citizens in Massachusetts willing to act as judges and captors. Moreover, it discloses the secret of the new times, that Slavery was no longer mendicant, but was become aggressive and dangerous.

The way in which the country was dragged to consent to this, and the disastrous defection (on the miserable cry of Union) of the men of letters, of the colleges, of educated men, nay, of some preachers of religion,—was the darkest passage in the history. It showed that our prosperity had hurt us, and that we could not be shocked by crime. It showed that the old religion and the sense of the right had faded and gone out; that while we reckoned ourselves a highly cultivated nation, our bellies had run away with our brains, and the principles of culture and progress did not exist.

For I suppose that liberty is an accurate index, in men and nations, of general progress. The theory of personal liberty must always appeal to the most refined communities and to the men of the rarest perception and of delicate moral sense. For there are rights which rest on the finest sense of justice, and, with every degree of civility, it will be more truly felt and defined. A barbarous tribe of good stock will, by means of their best heads, secure substantial liberty. But where there is any weakness in a race, and it becomes in a degree matter of concession and protection from their stronger neighbors, the incompatibility and offensiveness of the wrong will of course be most evident to the most cultivated. For it is,—is it not?—the essence of courtesy, of politeness, of religion, of love, to prefer another, to postpone oneself, to protect another from oneself. That is the distinction of the gentleman, to defend the weak and redress the injured, as it is of the savage and the brutal to usurp and use others.

In Massachusetts, as we all know, there has always existed a predominant conservative spirit. We have more money and value of every kind than other people, and wish to keep them. The plea on which freedom was resisted was Union. I went to certain serious men, who had a little more reason than the rest, and inquired why they took this part? They answered that they had no confidence in their strength to resist the Democratic party; that they saw plainly that all was going to the utmost verge of licence; each was vying with his neighbor to lead the party, by proposing the worst measure, and they threw themselves on the extreme conservatism, as a drag on the wheel: that they knew Cuba would be had, and Mexico would be had, and they stood stiffly on conservatism, and as near to monarchy as they could, only to moderate the velocity with which the car was running down the precipice. In short, their theory was despair; the Whig wisdom was only reprieve, a waiting to be last devoured. They side with Carolina, or with Arkansas, only to make a show of Whig strength, wherewith to resist a little longer this general ruin.

I have a respect for conservatism. I know how deeply founded it is in our nature, and how idle are all attempts to shake ourselves free from it. We are all conservatives, half Whig, half Democrat, in our essences: and might as well try to jump out of our skins as to escape from our Whiggery. There are two forces in Nature, by whose antagonism we exist; the power of Fate, Fortune, the laws of the world, the order of things, or however else we choose to phrase it, the material necessities, on the one hand,—and Will or Duty or Freedom on the other.

May and Must, and the sense of right and duty, on the one hand, and the material necessities on the other: May and Must. In vulgar politics the Whig goes for what has been, for the old necessities,—the Musts. The reformer goes for the Better, for the ideal good, for the Mays. But each of these parties must of necessity take in, in some measure, the principles of the other. Each wishes to cover the whole ground; to hold fast *and* to advance. Only, one lays the emphasis on keeping, and the other on advancing. I too think the *musts* are a safe company to follow, and even agreeable. But if we are Whigs, let us be Whigs of nature and science, and so for all the necessities. Let us know that, over and above all the *musts* of poverty and appetite, is the instinct of man to rise, and the instinct to love and help his brother.

Now, Gentlemen, I think we have in this hour instruction again in the simplest lesson. Events roll, millions of men are engaged, and the result is the enforcing of some of those first commandments which we heard in the nursery. We never get beyond our first lesson, for, really, the world exists, as I understand it, to teach the science of liberty, which begins with liberty from fear.

The events of this month are teaching one thing plain and clear, the worthlessness of good tools to bad workmen; that official papers are of no use; resolutions of public meetings, platforms of conventions, no, nor laws, nor constitutions, any more. These are all declaratory of the will of the moment, and are passed with more levity and on grounds far less honorable than ordinary business transactions of the street.

You relied on the constitution. It has not the word *slave* in it; and very good argument has shown that it would not warrant the crimes that are done under it; that, with provisions so vague for an object not named, and which could not be availed of to claim a barrel of sugar or a barrel of corn, the robbing of a man and of all his posterity is effected. You relied on the Supreme Court. The law was right, excellent law for the lambs. But what if unhappily the judges were chosen from the wolves, and give to all the law a wolfish interpretation? You relied on the Missouri Compromise. That is ridden over. You relied on State sovereignty in the Free States to protect their citizens. They are driven with contempt out of the courts and out of the territory of the Slave States,—if they are so happy as to get out with their lives,—and now you relied on these dismal guaranties infamously made in 1850; and, before the body of Webster is yet crumbled, it is found that they have crumbled. This eternal monument of his fame and of the Union is rotten in four years. They are no guaranty to the free states. They are a guaranty to the slave states that, as they have hitherto met with no repulse, they shall meet with none.

I fear there is no reliance to be put on any kind or form of covenant, no, not on sacred forms, none on churches, none on bibles. For one would have said that a Christian would not keep slaves;—but the Christians keep slaves. Of course they will not dare to read the Bible? Won't they? They quote the Bible, quote Paul, quote Christ, to justify slavery. If slavery is good, then is lying, theft, arson, homicide, each and all good, and to be maintained by Union societies.

These things show that no forms, neither constitutions, nor laws, nor covenants, nor churches, nor bibles, are of any use in themselves. The Devil nestles comfortably into them all. There is no help but in the head and heart and hamstrings of a man. Covenants are of no use without honest men to keep them; laws of none but with loyal citizens to obey them. To interpret Christ it needs Christ in the heart. The teachings of the Spirit can be apprehended only by the same spirit that gave them forth. To make good the cause of Freedom, you must draw off from all foolish trust in others. You must be citadels and warriors yourselves, declarations of Independence, the charter, the battle and the victory. Cromwell said, "We can only resist the superior training of the King's soldiers, by enlisting godly men." And no man has a right to hope that the laws of New York will defend him from the contamination of slaves another day until he has made up his mind that he will not owe his protection to the laws of New York, but to his own sense and spirit. Then he protects New York. He only who is able to stand alone is qualified for society. And that I understand to be the end for which a soul exists in this world,—to be himself the counterbalance of all falsehood and all wrong. "The army of unright is encamped from pole to pole, but the road of victory is known to the just." Everything may be taken away; he may be poor, he may be houseless, yet he will know out of his arms to make a pillow, and out of his breast a bolster. Why have the minority no influence? Because they have not a real minority of one.

I conceive that thus to detach a man and make him feel that he is to owe all to himself, is the way to make him strong and rich; and here the optimist must find, if anywhere, the benefit of Slavery. We have many teachers; we are in this world for culture, to be instructed in realities, in the laws of moral and intelligent nature; and our education is not conducted by toys and luxuries, but by austere and rugged masters, by poverty, solitude, passions, War, Slavery; to know that Paradise is under the shadow of swords; that divine sentiments which are always soliciting us are breathed into us from on high, and are an offset to a Universe of suffering and crime; that self-reliance, the height and perfection of man, is reliance on God. The insight of the religious sentiment will disclose to him unexpected aids in the nature of things. The Persian Saadi said, "Beware of hurting the orphan. When the orphan sets a-crying, the throne of the Almighty is rocked from side to side."

Whenever a man has come to this mind, that there is no Church for him but his believing prayer; no Constitution but his dealing well and justly with his neighbor; no liberty but his invincible will to do right,—then certain aids and allies will promptly appear: for the constitution of the Universe is on his side. It is of no use to vote down gravitation of morals. What is useful will last, whilst that which is hurtful to the world will sink beneath all the opposing forces which it must exasperate. The terror which the Marseillaise struck into oppression, it thunders again to-day,—

"Tout est soldat pour vous combattre."

Everything turns soldier to fight you down. The end for which man was made is not crime in any form, and a man cannot steal without incurring the penalties of the thief, though all the legislatures vote that it is virtuous, and though there be a general conspiracy among scholars and official persons to hold him up, and to say, *"Nothing is good but stealing.*" A man who commits a crime defeats the end of his existence. He was created for benefit, and he exists for harm; and as well-doing makes power and wisdom, ill-doing takes them away. A man who steals another man's labor steals away his own faculties; his integrity, his humanity is flowing away from him. The habit of oppression cuts out the moral eyes, and, though the intellect goes on simulating the moral as before, its sanity is gradually destroyed. It takes away the presentiments.

I suppose in general this is allowed, that if you have a nice question of right and wrong, you would not go with it to Louis Napoleon, or to a political hack, or to a slave-driver. The habit of mind of traders in power would not be esteemed favorable to delicate moral perception. American slavery affords no exception to this rule. No excess of good nature or of tenderness in individuals has been able to give a new character to the system, to tear down the whipping-house. The plea in the mouth of a slaveholder that the negro is an inferior race sounds very oddly in my ear. "The masters of slaves seem generally anxious to prove that they are not of a race superior in any noble quality to the meanest of their bondmen." And indeed when the Southerner points to the anatomy of the negro, and talks of chimpanzee,—I recall Montesquieu's remark, "It will not do to say that negroes are men, lest it should turn out that whites are not."

Slavery is disheartening; but Nature is not so helpless but it can rid itself at last of every wrong. But the spasms of Nature are centuries and ages, and will tax the faith of short-lived men. Slowly, slowly the Avenger comes, but comes surely. The proverbs of the nations affirm these delays, but affirm the arrival. They say, "God may consent, but not forever." The delay of the Divine Justice—this was the meaning and soul of the Greek Tragedy; this the soul of their religion. "There has come, too, one to whom lurking warfare is dear, Retribution, with a soul full of wiles; a violator of hospitality; guileful without the guilt of guile; limping, late in her arrival." They said of the happiness of the unjust, that "at its close it begets itself an offspring and does not die childless, and instead of good fortune, there sprouts forth for posterity ever-ravening calamity:"—

"For evil word shall evil word be said,
For murder-stroke a murder-stroke be paid.
Who smites must smart."

These delays, you see them now in the temper of the times. The national spirit in this country is so drowsy, preoccupied with interest, deaf to principle. The Anglo-Saxon race is proud and strong and selfish. They believe only in Anglo-Saxons. In 1825 Greece found America deaf, Poland found America deaf, Italy and Hungary found her deaf. England maintains trade, not liberty; stands against Greece; against Hungary; against Schleswig-Holstein; against the French Republic whilst it was a republic.

To faint hearts the times offer no invitation, and torpor exists here throughout the active classes on the subject of domestic slavery and its appalling aggressions. Yes, that is the stern edict of Providence, that liberty shall be no hasty fruit, but that event on event, population on population, age on age, shall cast itself into the opposite scale, and not until liberty has slowly accumulated weight enough to countervail and preponderate against all this, can the sufficient recoil come. All the great cities, all the refined circles, all the statesmen, Guizot, Palmerston, Webster, Calhoun, are sure to be found befriending liberty with their words, and crushing it with their votes. Liberty is never cheap. It is made difficult, because freedom is the accomplishment and perfectness of man. He is a finished man; earning and bestowing good; equal to the world; at home in Nature and dignifying that; the sun does not see anything nobler, and has nothing to teach him. Therefore mountains of difficulty must be surmounted, stern trials met, wiles of seduction, dangers, healed by a quarantine of calamities to measure his strength before he dare say, I am free.

Whilst the inconsistency of slavery with the principles on which the world is built guarantees its downfall, I own that the patience it requires is almost too sublime for mortals, and seems to demand of us more than mere hoping. And when one sees how fast the rot spreads,—it is growing serious,—I think we demand of superior men that they be superior in this,—that the mind and the virtue shall give their verdict in their day, and accelerate so far the progress of civilization. Possession is sure to throw its stupid strength for existing power, and appetite and ambition will go for that. Let the aid of virtue, intelligence and education be cast where they rightfully belong. They are organically ours. Let them be loyal to their own. I wish to see the instructed class here know their own flag, and not fire on their comrades. We should not forgive the clergy for taking on every issue the immoral side; nor the Bench, if it put itself on the side of the culprit; nor the Government, if it sustain the mob against the laws.

It is a potent support and ally to a brave man standing single, or with a few, for the right, and out-voted and ostracized, to know that better men in other parts of the country appreciate the service and will rightly report him to his own and the next age. Without this assurance, he will sooner sink. He may well say, 'If my countrymen do not care to be defended, I too will decline the controversy, from which I only reap invectives and hatred.' Yet the lovers of liberty may with reason tax the coldness and indifferentism of scholars and literary men. They are lovers of liberty in Greece and Rome and in the English Commonwealth, but they are lukewarm lovers of the liberty of America in 1854. The universities are not, as in Hobbes's time, "the core of rebellion," no, but the seat of inertness. They have forgotten their allegiance to the Muse, and grown worldly and political. I listened, lately, on one of those occasions when the university chooses one of its distinguished sons returning from the political arena, believing that senators and statesmen would be glad to throw off the harness and to dip again in the Castalian pools. But if audiences forget themselves, statesmen do not. The low bows to all the crockery gods of the day were duly made:— only in one part of the discourse the orator allowed to transpire, rather against his will, a little sober sense. It was this: 'I am, as you see, a man virtuously inclined, and only corrupted by my profession of politics. I should prefer the right side. You, gentlemen of these literary and scientific schools, and the important class you represent, have the power to make your verdict clear and prevailing. Had you done so, you would have found me its glad organ and champion. Abstractly, I should have preferred that side. But you have not done it. You have not spoken out. You have failed to arm me. I can only deal with masses as I find them. Abstractions are not for me. I go then for such parties and opinions as have provided me with a working apparatus. I give you my word, not without regret, that I was first for you; and though I am now to deny and condemn you, you see it is not my will but the party necessity.' Having made this manifesto and professed his adoration for liberty in the time of his grandfathers, he proceeded with his work of denouncing freedom and freemen at the present day, much in the tone and spirit in which Lord Bacon prosecuted his benefactor Essex. He denounced every name and aspect under which liberty and progress dare show themselves in this age and country, but with a lingering conscience which qualified each sentence with a recommendation to mercy.

But I put it to every noble and generous spirit, to every poetic, every heroic, every religious heart, that not so is our learning, our education, our poetry, our worship to be declared. Liberty is aggressive, Liberty is the Crusade of all brave and conscientious men, the Epic Poetry, the new religion, the chivalry of all gentlemen. This is the oppressed Lady whom true knights on their oath and honor must rescue and save.

Now at last we are disenchanted and shall have no more false hopes. I respect the Anti-Slavery Society. It is the Cassandra that has foretold all that has befallen, fact for fact, years ago; foretold all, and no man laid it to heart. It seemed, as the Turks say, "Fate makes that a man should not believe his own eyes." But the Fugitive Law did much to unglue the eyes of men, and now the Nebraska Bill leaves us staring. The Anti-Slavery Society will add many members this year. The Whig Party will join it; the Democrats will join it. The population of the free states will join it. I doubt not, at last, the slave states will join it. But be that sooner or later, and whoever comes or stays away, I hope we have reached the end of our unbelief, have come to a belief that there is a divine Providence in the world, which will not save us but through our own coöperation.

THOREAU, "SLAVERY IN MASSACHUSETTS" (1854)

At the beginning of his 1851 "The Fugitive Slave Law" speech, Emerson remarked that his outdoor time was ruined by "ignominy which has fallen on Massachusetts" that robbed "the landscape of its beauty" and took "sunshine out of every hour." More famously, in "Slavery in Massachusetts" Thoreau stated the "memory of my country spoils my walk." This would seem a weak antislavery argument, unless you've read Thoreau's 1862 "Walking," his last published essay before his death.

"Walking" was given as a lyceum lecture in the 1850s, and so Thoreau's views evolved along with his daily walks, or saunters, as he called them. To saunter is to intentionally lose the world, along with our personal worries, returning to the roots of self and our place within nature. He witnessed encroaching industrialization, and increased tameness, in Concord and Boston, and sauntered west to find what was more wild and free, which he experienced as a healing tonic. For slavery to spoil his walk, then, is to take away his source of sanity.

Slavery is ethically insane and was driving Thoreau crazy. Just like Emerson let loose against the institution of slavery and Daniel Webster in "The Fugitive Slave Law" speeches, Thoreau let loose against the institution of slavery and the State of Massachusetts and its functionaries in "Slavery in Massachusetts." Both became more radical; but that raises the question: what does it mean to be radical? We must question the definition of radicalism, or extremism for that matter. What could be more radical and extreme than the enslavement of fellow humans, fellow Thous, based on skin color? In our time, what could be more radical and extreme than the heating of the whole planet upon which we depend for survival and treating humans, especially people of color and the poor, and nonhumans in the sixth "great" period of species extirpation, as a collection of Its or objects?

To be radical, etymologically, is to go to the roots. Emerson and Thoreau argued that we must go to the roots of eco-social evils and our despair, and thus the roots of I-It economics and attitudes that undergird those evils and our despair. Given the unjust radicalism of slavery, it is head-logical but also heart-necessary to have a radical response. The same is true for climate crisis and injustice.

For Thoreau, sauntering is spiritual because we need to lose our little selves to find a wider self and world, and radical because such finding engenders responsibility, the call to listen and act. His walks, then, were not just spoiled, but were catalysts to speaking out. And speak out he did in his "Slavery in Massachusetts" address at an anti-slavery rally at the Harmony Grove amphitheater in South Framingham, MA in defense of Anthony Burns and all escaped slaves and all who remained enslaved.

Thoreau followed notable speakers such as Sojourner Truth, Wendell Phillips, and William Garrison, who opened the event by burning the Constitution. At the end of his speech, Thoreau somewhat surprisingly returned to nature in the form of a white water-lily, "an emblem of purity" that signified hope. The beautiful water-lily emerged from the "slime and muck of the earth." Might virtuous humans emerge from "sloth and vice" and "the decay of humanity"? Like his call to conscience in "Civil Disobedience," that question, and several searing denunciations from his address, reverberate down through the centuries.

SOURCES

Emerson, Ralph Waldo & Henry David Thoreau. *Nature/Walking*. Edited by John Elder. Boston: Beacon Press, 1991.

Thoreau, Henry David. *The Portable Thoreau*. Edited by Carl Bode. New York: Penguin Books, 1975.

Walls, Laura Dassow. *Henry David Thoreau: A Life*. Chicago: The University of Chicago Press, 2017.

SLAVERY IN MASSACHUSETTS
(1854)

Henry David Thoreau

I lately attended a meeting of the citizens of Concord, expecting, as one among many, to speak on the subject of slavery in Massachusetts; but I was surprised and disappointed to find that what had called my townsmen together was the destiny of Nebraska, and not of Massachusetts, and that what I had to say would be entirely out of order. I had thought that the house was on fire, and not the prairie; but though several of the citizens of Massachusetts are now in prison for attempting to rescue a slave from her own clutches, not one of the speakers at that meeting expressed regret for it, not one even referred to it. It was only the disposition of some wild lands a thousand miles off which appeared to concern them. The inhabitants of Concord are not prepared to stand by one of their own bridges, but talk only of taking up a position on the highlands beyond the Yellowstone River. Our Buttricks and Davises and Hosmers are retreating thither, and I fear that they will leave no Lexington Common between them and the enemy. There is not one slave in Nebraska; there are perhaps a million slaves in Massachusetts.

They who have been bred in the school of politics fail now and always to face the facts. Their measures are half measures and makeshifts merely. They put off the day of settlement indefinitely, and meanwhile the debt accumulates. Though the Fugitive Slave Law had not been the subject of discussion on that occasion, it was at length faintly resolved by my townsmen, at an adjourned meeting, as I learn, that the compromise compact of 1820 having been repudiated by one of the parties, "Therefore,... the Fugitive Slave Law of 1850 must be repealed." But this is not the reason why an iniquitous law should be repealed. The fact which the politician faces is merely that there is less honor among thieves than was supposed, and not the fact that they are thieves. As I had no opportunity to express my thoughts at that meeting, will you allow me to do so here?

Again it happens that the Boston Court-House is full of armed men, holding prisoner and trying a MAN, to find out if he is not really a SLAVE. Does any one think that justice or God awaits Mr. Loring's decision? For him to sit there deciding still, when this question is already decided from eternity to eternity, and the unlettered slave himself and the multitude around have long since heard and assented to the decision, is simply to make himself ridiculous. We may be tempted to ask from whom he received his commission, and who he is that received it; what novel statutes he obeys, and what precedents are to him of authority. Such an arbiter's very existence is an impertinence. We do not ask him to make up his mind, but to make up his pack.

I listen to hear the voice of a Governor, Commander-in-Chief of the forces of Massachusetts. I hear only the creaking of crickets and the hum of insects which now fill the summer air. The Governor's exploit is to review the troops on muster days. I have seen him on horseback, with his hat off, listening to a chaplain's prayer. It chances that

that is all I have ever seen of a Governor. I think that I could manage to get along without one. If he is not of the least use to prevent my being kidnapped, pray of what important use is he likely to be to me? When freedom is most endangered, he dwells in the deepest obscurity. A distinguished clergyman told me that he chose the profession of a clergyman because it afforded the most leisure for literary pursuits. I would recommend to him the profession of a Governor.

Three years ago, also, when the Sims tragedy was acted, I said to myself, There is such an officer, if not such a man, as the Governor of Massachusetts—what has he been about the last fortnight? Has he had as much as he could do to keep on the fence during this moral earthquake? It seemed to me that no keener satire could have been aimed at, no more cutting insult have been offered to that man, than just what happened—the absence of all inquiry after him in that crisis. The worst and the most I chance to know of him is that he did not improve that opportunity to make himself known, and worthily known. He could at least have resigned himself into fame. It appeared to be forgotten that there was such a man or such an office. Yet no doubt he was endeavoring to fill the gubernatorial chair all the while. He was no Governor of mine. He did not govern me.

But at last, in the present case, the Governor was heard from. After he and the United States government had perfectly succeeded in robbing a poor innocent black man of his liberty for life, and, as far as they could, of his Creator's likeness in his breast, he made a speech to his accomplices, at a congratulatory supper!

I have read a recent law of this State, making it penal for any officer of the "Commonwealth" to "detain or aid in the...

detention," anywhere within its limits, "of any person, for the reason that he is claimed as a fugitive slave." Also, it was a matter of notoriety that a writ of replevin to take the fugitive out of the custody of the United States Marshal could not be served for want of sufficient force to aid the officer.

I had thought that the Governor was, in some sense, the executive officer of the State; that it was his business, as a Governor, to see that the laws of the State were executed; while, as a man, he took care that he did not, by so doing, break the laws of humanity; but when there is any special important use for him, he is useless, or worse than useless, and permits the laws of the State to go unexecuted. Perhaps I do not know what are the duties of a Governor; but if to be a Governor requires to subject one's self to so much ignominy without remedy, if it is to put a restraint upon my manhood, I shall take care never to be Governor of Massachusetts. I have not read far in the statutes of this Commonwealth. It is not profitable reading. They do not always say what is true; and they do not always mean what they say. What I am concerned to know is, that that man's influence and authority were on the side of the slaveholder, and not of the slave- of the guilty, and not of the innocent- of injustice, and not of justice. I never saw him of whom I speak; indeed, I did not know that he was Governor until this event occurred. I heard of him and Anthony Burns at the same time, and thus, undoubtedly, most will hear of him. So far am I from being governed by him. I do not mean that it was anything to his discredit that I had not heard of him, only that I heard what I did. The worst I shall say of him is, that he proved no better than the majority of his constituents would be likely to prove. In my opinion, be was not equal to the occasion.

The whole military force of the State is at the service of a Mr. Suttle, a slaveholder from Virginia, to enable him to catch a man whom he calls his property; but not a soldier is offered to save a citizen of Massachusetts from being kidnapped! Is this what all these soldiers, all this training, have been for these seventy-nine years past? Have they been trained merely to rob Mexico and carry back fugitive slaves to their masters?

These very nights I heard the sound of a drum in our streets. There were men training still; and for what? I could with an effort pardon the cockerels of Concord for crowing still, for they, perchance, had not been beaten that morning; but I could not excuse this rub-a-dub of the "trainers." The slave was carried back by exactly such as these; i.e., by the soldier, of whom the best you can say in this connection is that he is a fool made conspicuous by a painted coat.

Three years ago, also, just a week after the authorities of Boston assembled to carry back a perfectly innocent man, and one whom they knew to be innocent, into slavery, the inhabitants of Concord caused the bells to be rung and the cannons to be fired, to celebrate their liberty—and the courage and love of liberty of their ancestors who fought at the bridge. As if those three millions had fought for the right to be free themselves, but to hold in slavery three million others. Nowadays, men wear a fool's-cap, and call it a liberty-cap. I do not know but there are some who, if they were tied to a whipping-post, and could but get one hand free, would use it to ring the bells and fire the cannons to celebrate their liberty. So some of my townsmen took the liberty to ring and fire. That was the extent of their freedom; and when the sound of the bells died away, their liberty died away also; when the powder was all expended, their liberty went off with the smoke.

The joke could be no broader if the inmates of the prisons were to subscribe for all the powder to be used in such salutes, and hire the jailers to do the firing and ringing for them, while they enjoyed it through the grating.

This is what I thought about my neighbors.

Every humane and intelligent inhabitant of Concord, when he or she heard those bells and those cannons, thought not with pride of the events of the 19th of April, 1775, but with shame of the events of the 12th of April, 1851. But now we have half buried that old shame under a new one.

Massachusetts sat waiting Mr. Loring's decision, as if it could in any way affect her own criminality. Her crime, the most conspicuous and fatal crime of all, was permitting him to be the umpire in such a case. It was really the trial of Massachusetts. Every moment that she hesitated to set this man free, every moment that she now hesitates to atone for her crime, she is convicted. The Commissioner on her case is God; not Edward G. God, but simply God.

I wish my countrymen to consider, that whatever the human law may be, neither an individual nor a nation can ever commit the least act of injustice against the obscurest individual without having to pay the penalty for it. A government which deliberately enacts injustice, and persists in it, will at length even become the laughing-stock of the world.

Much has been said about American slavery, but I think that we do not even yet realize what slavery is. If I were seriously to propose to Congress to make mankind into sausages, I have no doubt that most of the members would smile at my proposition, and if any believed me to be in earnest, they would think that I proposed something much worse than Congress had ever done. But if any of them will tell me that to make a man into a sausage would be much worse,—would be any worse, than to make him into a slave,—than it was to enact the Fugitive Slave Law, I will accuse him of foolishness, of intellectual incapacity, of making a distinction without a difference. The one is just as sensible a proposition as the other.

I hear a good deal said about trampling this law under foot. Why, one need not go out of his way to do that. This law rises not to the level of the head or the reason; its natural habitat is in the dirt. It was born and bred, and has its life, only in the dust and mire, on a level with the feet; and he who walks with freedom, and does not with Hindoo mercy avoid treading on every venomous reptile, will inevitably tread on it, and so trample it under foot—and Webster, its maker, with it, like the dirt—bug and its ball.

Recent events will be valuable as a criticism on the administration of justice in our midst, or, rather, as showing what are the true resources of justice in any community. It has come to this, that the friends of liberty, the friends of the slave, have shuddered when they have understood that his fate was left to the legal tribunals of the country to be decided. Free men have no faith that justice will be awarded in such a case. The judge may decide this way or that; it is a kind of accident, at best. It is evident that he is not a competent authority in so important a case. It is no time, then, to be judging according to his precedents, but to establish a precedent for the future. I would much rather trust to the sentiment of the people. In their vote you would get something of some value, at least, however small; but in the other case, only the trammeled judgment of an individual, of no significance, be it which way it might.

It is to some extent fatal to the courts, when the people are compelled to go behind them. I do not wish to believe that the courts were made for fair weather, and for very civil cases merely; but think of leaving it to any court in the land to decide whether more than three millions of people, in this case a sixth part of a nation, have a right to be freemen or not! But it has been left to the courts of justice, so called—to the Supreme Court of the land—and, as you all know, recognizing no authority but the Constitution, it has decided that the three millions are and shall continue to be slaves. Such judges as these are merely the inspectors of a pick-lock and murderer's tools, to tell him whether they are in working order or not, and there they think that their responsibility ends. There was a prior case on the docket, which they, as judges appointed by God, had no right to skip; which having been justly settled, they would have been saved from this humiliation. It was the case of the murderer himself.

The law will never make men free; it is men who have got to make the law free. They are the lovers of law and order who observe the law when the government breaks it.

Among human beings, the judge whose words seal the fate of a man furthest into eternity is not he who merely pronounces the verdict of the law, but he, whoever he may be, who, from a love of truth, and unprejudiced by any custom or enactment of men, utters a true opinion or sentence concerning him. He it is that sentences him. Whoever can discern truth has received his commission from a higher source than the chiefest justice in the world who can discern only law. He finds himself constituted judge of the judge. Strange that it should be necessary to state such simple truths!

I am more and more convinced that, with reference to any public question, it is more important to know what the country thinks of it than what the city thinks. The city does not think much. On any moral question, I would rather have the opinion of Boxboro than of Boston and New York put together. When the former speaks, I feel as if somebody had spoken, as if humanity was yet, and a reasonable being had asserted its rights,—as if some unprejudiced men among the country's hills had at length turned their attention to the subject, and by a few sensible words redeemed the reputation of the race. When, in some obscure country town, the farmers come together to a special town-meeting, to express their opinion on some subject which is vexing the land, that, I think, is the true Congress, and the most respectable one that is ever assembled in the United States.

It is evident that there are, in this Commonwealth at least, two parties, becoming more and more distinct—the party of the city, and the party of the country. I know that the country is mean enough, but I am glad to believe that there is a slight difference in her favor. But as yet she has few, if any organs, through which to express herself. The editorials which she reads, like the news, come from the seaboard. Let us, the inhabitants of the country, cultivate self-respect. Let us not send to the city for aught more essential than our broadcloths and groceries; or, if we read the opinions of the city, let us entertain opinions of our own.

Among measures to be adopted, I would suggest to make as earnest and vigorous an assault on the press as has already been made, and with effect, on the church. The church has much improved within a few years; but the press is, almost without exception, corrupt. I believe that in this country the press exerts a greater and a more pernicious influence than the church did in its worst period. We are not a religious people, but we are a nation of politicians. We do not care for the Bible, but we do care for the newspaper. At any meeting of politicians—like that at Concord the other evening, for instance—how impertinent it would be to quote from the Bible! how pertinent to quote from a newspaper or from the Constitution! The newspaper is a Bible which we read every morning and every afternoon, standing and sitting, riding and walking. It is a Bible which every man carries in his pocket, which lies on every table and counter, and which the mail, and thousands of missionaries, are continually dispersing. It is, in short, the only book which America has printed and which America reads. So wide is its influence. The editor is a preacher whom you voluntarily support. Your tax is commonly one cent daily, and it costs nothing for pew hire. But how many of these preachers preach the truth? I repeat the testimony of many an intelligent foreigner, as well as my own convictions, when I say, that probably no country was ever rubled by so mean a class of tyrants as, with a few noble exceptions, are the editors of the periodical press in this country. And as they live and rule only by their servility, and appealing to the worse, and not the better, nature of man, the people who read them are in the condition of the dog that returns to his vomit.

The Liberator and the Commonwealth were the only papers in Boston, as far as I know, which made themselves heard in condemnation of the cowardice and meanness of the authorities of that city, as exhibited in '51. The other journals, almost without exception, by their manner of referring to and speaking of the Fugitive Slave Law, and the carrying back of the slave Sims, insulted the common sense of the country, at least. And, for the most part, they did this, one would say, because they thought so to secure the approbation of their patrons, not being aware that a sounder sentiment prevailed to any extent in the heart of the Commonwealth. I am told that some of them have improved of late; but they are still eminently time-serving. Such is the character they have won.

But, thank fortune, this preacher can be even more easily reached by the weapons of the reformer than could the recreant priest. The free men of New England have only to refrain from purchasing and reading these sheets, have only to withhold their cents, to kill a score of them at once. One whom I respect told me that he purchased Mitchell's Citizen in the cars, and then throw it out the window. But would not his contempt have been more fatally expressed if he had not bought it?

Are they Americans? are they New Englanders? are they inhabitants of Lexington and Concord and Framingham, who read and support the Boston Post, Mail, Journal, Advertiser, Courier, and Times? Are these the Flags of our Union? I am not a newspaper reader, and may omit to name the worst.

Could slavery suggest a more complete servility than some of these journals exhibit? Is there any dust which their conduct does not lick, and make fouler still with its slime? I do not know whether the Boston Herald is still in existence, but I remember to have seen it about the streets when Sims was carried off. Did it not act its part well—serve its master faithfully! How could it have gone lower on its belly? How can a man stoop lower than he is low? do more than put his extremities in the place of the head he has? than make his head his lower extremity? When I have taken up this paper with my cuffs turned up, I have heard the gurgling of the sewer through every column. I have felt that I was handling a paper picked out of the public gutters, a leaf from the gospel of the gambling-house, the groggery, and the brothel, harmonizing with the gospel of the Merchants' Exchange.

The majority of the men of the North, and of the South and East and West, are not men of principle. If they vote, they do not send men to Congress on errands of humanity; but while their brothers and sisters are being scourged and hung for loving liberty, while—I might here insert all that slavery implies and is—it is the mismanagement of wood and iron and stone and gold which concerns them. Do what you will, O Government, with my wife and children, my mother and brother, my father and sister, I will obey your commands to the letter. It will indeed grieve me if you hurt them, if you deliver them to overseers to be hunted by bounds or to be whipped to death; but, nevertheless, I will peaceably pursue my chosen calling on this fair earth, until perchance, one day, when I have put on mourning for them dead, I shall have persuaded you to relent. Such is the attitude, such are the words of Massachusetts.

Rather than do thus, I need not say what match I would touch, what system endeavor to blow up; but as I love my life, I would side with the light, and let the dark earth roll from under me, calling my mother and my brother to follow.

I would remind my countrymen that they are to be men first, and Americans only at a late and convenient hour. No matter how valuable law may be to protect your property, even to keep soul and body together, if it do not keep you and humanity together.

I am sorry to say that I doubt if there is a judge in Massachusetts who is prepared to resign his office, and get his living innocently, whenever it is required of him to pass sentence under a law which is merely contrary to the law of God. I am compelled to see that they put themselves, or rather are by character, in this respect, exactly on a level with the marine who discharges his musket in any direction he is ordered to. They are just as much tools, and as little men. Certainly, they are not the more to be respected, because their master enslaves their understandings and consciences, instead of their bodies.

The judges and lawyers—simply as such, I mean—and all men of expediency, try this case by a very low and incompetent standard. They consider, not whether the Fugitive Slave Law is right, but whether it is what they call constitutional. Is virtue constitutional, or vice? Is equity constitutional, or iniquity? In important moral and vital questions, like this, it is just as impertinent to ask whether a law is constitutional or not, as to ask whether it is profitable or not. They persist in being the servants of the worst of men, and not the servants of humanity. The question is, not whether you or your grandfather, seventy years ago, did not enter into an agreement to serve the Devil, and that service is not accordingly now due; but whether you will not now, for once and at last, serve God—in spite of your own past recreancy, or that of your ancestor—by obeying that eternal and only just CONSTITUTION, which He, and not any Jefferson or Adams, has written in your being.

The amount of it is, if the majority vote the Devil to be God, the minority will live and behave accordingly—and obey the successful candidate, trusting that, some time or other, by some Speaker's casting—vote, perhaps, they may reinstate God. This is the highest principle I can get out or invent for my neighbors. These men act as if they believed that they could safely slide down a hill a little way—or a good way—and would surely come to a place, by and by, where they could begin to slide up again. This is expediency, or choosing that course which offers the slightest obstacles to the feet, that is, a downhill one. But there is no such thing as accomplishing a righteous reform by the use of "expediency." There is no such thing as sliding up hill. In morals the only sliders are backsliders.

Thus we steadily worship Mammon, both school and state and church, and on the seventh day curse God with a tintamar from one end of the Union to the other.

Will mankind never learn that policy is not morality—that it never secures any moral right, but considers merely what is expedient? chooses the available candidate—who is invariably the Devil—and what right have his constituents to be surprised, because the Devil does not behave like an angel of light? What is wanted is men, not of policy, but of probity—who recognize a higher law than the Constitution, or the decision of the majority. The fate of the country does not depend on how you vote at the polls—the worst man is as strong as the best at that game; it does not depend on what kind of paper you drop into the ballot—box once a year, but on what kind of man you drop from your chamber into the street every morning.

What should concern Massachusetts is not the Nebraska Bill, nor the Fugitive Slave Bill, but her own slaveholding and servility. Let the State dissolve her union with the slaveholder. She may wriggle and hesitate, and ask leave to read the Constitution once more; but she can find no respectable law or precedent which sanctions the continuance of such a union for an instant.

Let each inhabitant of the State dissolve his union with her, as long as she delays to do her duty.

The events of the past month teach me to distrust Fame. I see that she does not finely discriminate, but coarsely hurrahs. She considers not the simple heroism of an action, but only as it is connected with its apparent consequences. She praises till she is hoarse the easy exploit of the Boston tea party, but will be comparatively silent about the braver and more disinterestedly heroic attack on the Boston Court-House, simply because it was unsuccessful!

Covered with disgrace, the State has sat down coolly to try for their lives and liberties the men who attempted to do its duty for it. And this is called justice! They who have shown that they can behave particularly well may perchance be put under bonds for their good behavior. They whom truth requires at present to plead guilty are, of all the inhabitants of the State, preeminently innocent. While the Governor, and the Mayor, and countless officers of the Commonwealth are at large, the champions of liberty are imprisoned.

Only they are guiltless who commit the crime of contempt of such a court. It behooves every man to see that his influence is on the side of justice, and let the courts make their own characters. My sympathies in this case are wholly with the accused, and wholly against their accusers and judges. Justice is sweet and musical; but injustice is harsh and discordant. The judge still sits grinding at his organ, but it yields no music, and we hear only the sound of the handle. He believes that all the music resides in the handle, and the crowd toss him their coppers the same as before.

Do you suppose that that Massachusetts which is now doing these things—which hesitates to crown these men, some of whose lawyers, and even judges, perchance, may be driven to take refuge in some poor quibble, that they may not wholly outrage their instinctive sense of justice—do you suppose that she is anything but base and servile? that she is the champion of liberty?

Show me a free state, and a court truly of justice, and I will fight for them, if need be; but show me Massachusetts, and I refuse her my allegiance, and express contempt for her courts.

The effect of a good government is to make life more valuable—of a bad one, to make it less valuable. We can afford that railroad and all merely material stock should lose some of its value, for that only compels us to live more simply and economically; but suppose that the value of life itself should be diminished! How can we make a less demand on man and nature, how live more economically in respect to virtue and all noble qualities, than we do? I have lived for the last month—and I think that every man in Massachusetts capable of the sentiment of patriotism must have had a similar experience—with the sense of having suffered a vast and indefinite loss. I did not know at first what ailed me. At last it occurred to me that what I had lost was a country. I had never respected the government near to which I lived, but I had foolishly thought that I might manage to live here, minding my private affairs, and forget it. For my part, my old and worthiest pursuits have lost I cannot say how much of their attraction, and I feel that my investment in life here is worth many per cent less since Massachusetts last deliberately sent back an innocent man, Anthony Burns, to slavery. I dwelt before, perhaps, in the illusion that my life passed somewhere only between heaven and hell, but now I cannot persuade myself that I do not dwell wholly within hell. The site of that political organization called Massachusetts is to me morally covered with volcanic scoriae and cinders, such as Milton describes in the infernal regions. If there is any hell more unprincipled than our rulers, and we, the ruled, I feel curious to see it. Life itself being worth less, all things with it, which minister to it, are worth less. Suppose you have a small library, with pictures to adorn the walls—a garden laid out around—and contemplate scientific and literary pursuits and discover all at once that your villa, with all its contents is located in hell, and that the justice of the peace has a cloven foot and a forked tail—do not these things suddenly lose their value in your eyes?

 I feel that, to some extent, the State has fatally interfered with my lawful business. It has not only interrupted me in my passage through Court Street on errands of trade, but it has interrupted me and every man on his onward and upward path, on which he had trusted soon to leave Court Street far behind. What right had it to remind me of Court Street? I have found that hollow which even I had relied on for solid.

I am surprised to see men going about their business as if nothing had happened. I say to myself, "Unfortunates! they have not heard the news." I am surprised that the man whom I just met on horseback should be so earnest to overtake his newly bought cows running away—since all property is insecure, and if they do not run away again, they may be taken away from him when he gets them. Fool! does he not know that his seed-corn is worth less this year—that all beneficent harvests fail as you approach the empire of hell? No prudent man will build a stone house under these circumstances, or engage in any peaceful enterprise which it requires a long time to accomplish. Art is as long as ever, but life is more interrupted and less available for a man's proper pursuits. It is not an era of repose. We have used up all our inherited freedom. If we would save our lives, we must fight for them.

I walk toward one of our ponds; but what signifies the beauty of nature when men are base? We walk to lakes to see our serenity reflected in them; when we are not serene, we go not to them. Who can be serene in a country where both the rulers and the ruled are without principle? The remembrance of my country spoils my walk. My thoughts are murder to the State, and involuntarily go plotting against her.

But it chanced the other day that I scented a white water-lily, and a season I had waited for had arrived. It is the emblem of purity. It bursts up so pure and fair to the eye, and so sweet to the scent, as if to show us what purity and sweetness reside in, and can be extracted from, the slime and muck of earth. I think I have plucked the first one that has opened for a mile. What confirmation of our hopes is in the

Thoreau, "Slavery in Massachusetts" (1854)

fragrance of this flower! I shall not so soon despair of the world for it, notwithstanding slavery, and the cowardice and want of principle of Northern men. It suggests what kind of laws have prevailed longest and widest, and still prevail, and that the time may come when man's deeds will smell as sweet. Such is the odor which the plant emits. If Nature can compound this fragrance still annually, I shall believe her still young and full of vigor, her integrity and genius unimpaired, and that there is virtue even in man, too, who is fitted to perceive and love it. It reminds me that Nature has been partner to no Missouri Compromise. I scent no compromise in the fragrance of the water-lily. It is not a *Nymphaea Douglasii*. In it, the sweet, and pure, and innocent are wholly sundered from the obscene and baleful. I do not scent in this the time—serving irresolution of a Massachusetts Governor, nor of a Boston Mayor. So behave that the odor of your actions may enhance the general sweetness of the atmosphere, that when we behold or scent a flower, we may not be reminded how inconsistent your deeds are with it; for all odor is but one form of advertisement of a moral quality, and if fair actions had not been performed, the lily would not smell sweet. The foul slime stands for the sloth and vice of man, the decay of humanity; the fragrant flower that springs from it, for the purity and courage which are immortal.

Slavery and servility have produced no sweet-scented flower annually, to charm the senses of men, for they have no real life: they are merely a decaying and a death, offensive to all healthy nostrils. We do not complain that they live, but that they do not get buried. Let the living bury them: even they are good for manure.

EMERSON, "JOHN BROWN" (1960)

Emerson's talks defending John Brown are less well known than Thoreau's defense in his two talks, "A Plea for Captain John Brown" and "The Last Days of John Brown." Emerson, though, was better known than Thoreau when Brown and his men raided the Harper's Ferry armory and had more influence with a broad audience. That influence was aided by his stellar reputation, as well as his more measured constitution, which made the public more likely to listen to him. And the public's willingness to listen to Emerson opened the door for them to listen to Thoreau and others. But not everyone listened. Emerson's radical turn also led him to face vitriolic audiences and be attacked by newspaper editors, and not just because he supported Brown but also years earlier after he castigated Daniel Webster.

In this relatively short talk in Salem, MA, Emerson provides biographical information on Brown, including an experience in his youth, in which he witnessed a friendly black boy who he liked and admired being horribly abused. This early experience led him to swear an oath to fight slavery, which played itself out at Harper's Ferry decades later. Emerson also praises his virtues, going as far as to say that he had no vices, or that he had "no vulgar trait." Such claims are the fount of a long-lasting controversy: many thought Brown a religious zealot who had to be mad to attack the armory. Even Emerson, who was surprised by the attack, initially remarked to his brother that "Brown is a true hero, but he lost his head there."

Brown's violence was considered a vice and condemned by pro-slavery Southerners but also by numerous anti-slavery Northerners, including the arch-abolitionist William Garrison. And that is without considering Brown's earlier violence at the Pottawatomie Massacre, in which he and his allies dragged five pro-slavery men out of their homes and shot and sliced them to a bloody death.

In an 1859 lecture in support of Brown's family, Emerson focuses on Brown the "true hero," once again praising his virtues and ignoring any vices, while arguing he followed the Golden Rule and Declaration of Independence to their logical conclusion. Emerson championed Brown as embodying transcendentalist principles, even though he was more Calvinist than transcendentalist. Brown sought to obey God's will, and slavery could not possibly be God's will. Emerson also saw Brown as Christ-like. In another 1859 lecture, "Courage," he stated that Brown "would make the gallows glorious like the cross." This fiery rhetoric inflamed divisiveness between North and South after it was printed widely in newspapers. Was it a spark that contributed to the fire that would be the Civil War?

The Civil War is a lot to lay on the hands, or words, of Emerson, or the hands or words of any individual. The reasons for the War are obviously far more complex, including the 1857 Dred Scott decision, in which the Supreme Court ruled that slaves were not citizens and thus had no legal protection under the Constitution. This decision stoked Brown's righteous anger and willingness to turn to violence. But Emerson and Thoreau's support of Brown, along with the support of other transcendentalists, most definitely had impact that helped to march differing factions of the young nation to battle. An estimated 750,000 would die in the Civil War. That is quite a number to consider. But so is another one: in 1860, there were approximately four million slaves.

SOURCES

Emerson, Ralph Waldo. *Emerson's Antislavery Writings*. Edited by Len Gougeon and Joel Myerson. New Haven: Yale University Press, 1995.

PBS. "John Brown's Holy War: Pottawatomie Massacre," *The American Experience*, February 28, 2000.

Reynold, David S. "Transcendentalism, Transnationalism, and Antislavery Violence: Concord's Embrace of John Brown." In *Emerson for the 21st Century*. Edited by Barry Tharaud. Delaware: University of Delaware Press, 2010.

JOHN BROWN

Ralph Waldo Emerson

[Speech at Salem, January 6, 1860]

A MAN there came, whence none could tell,
Bearing a touchstone in his hand,
And tested all things in the land
By its unerring spell.
A thousand transformations rose
From fair to foul, from foul to fair:
The golden crown he did not spare,
Nor scorn the beggar's clothes.
Then angrily the people cried,
The loss outweighs the profit far;
Our goods suffice us as they are:
'We will not have them tried.'
And since they could not so avail
To check his unrelenting quest,
They seized him, saying, 'Let him test
How real is our jail!'
But though they slew him with the sword,
And in the fire his touchstone burned,
Its doings could not be o'erturned,
Its undoings restored.
And when, to stop all future harm,
They strewed its ashes to the breeze,

They little guessed each grain of these
Conveyed the perfect charm."

—WILLIAM ALLINGHAM.

MR. CHAIRMAN: I have been struck with one fact, that the best orators who have added their praise to his fame,—and I need not go out of this house to find the purest eloquence in the country,—have one rival who comes off a little better, and that is John Brown. Everything that is said of him leaves people a little dissatisfied; but as soon as they read his own speeches and letters they are heartily contented,—such is the singleness of purpose which justifies him to the head and the heart of all. Taught by this experience, I mean, in the few remarks I have to make, to cling to his history, or let him speak for himself.

John Brown, the founder of liberty in Kansas, was born in Torrington, Litchfield County, Connecticut, in 1800. When he was five years old his father emigrated to Ohio, and the boy was there set to keep sheep and to look after cattle and dress skins; he went bareheaded and bare-footed, and clothed in buckskin. He said that he loved rough play, could never have rough play enough; could not see a seedy hat without wishing to pull it off. But for this it needed that the playmates should be equal; not one in fine clothes and the other in buckskin; not one his own master, hale and hearty, and the other watched and whipped. But it chanced that in Pennsylvania, where he was sent by his father to collect cattle, he fell in with a boy whom he heartily liked and whom he looked upon as his superior. This boy was a slave; he saw him beaten with an iron shovel, and otherwise maltreated; he saw that this boy had nothing better to look forward to in life, whilst he himself was petted and made much of; for he was much considered in the family where he then stayed, from the circumstance that this boy of twelve years had conducted alone a drove of cattle a hundred miles. But the colored boy had no friend, and no future. This worked such indignation in him that he swore an oath of resistance to slavery as long as he lived. And thus his enterprise to go into Virginia and run off five hundred or a thousand slaves was not a piece of spite or revenge, a plot of two years or of twenty years, but the keeping of an oath made to heaven and earth forty-seven years before. Forty-seven years at least, though I incline to accept his own account of the matter at Charlestown, which makes the date a little older, when he said, "This was all settled millions of years before the world was made."

He grew up a religious and manly person, in severe poverty; a fair specimen of the best stock of New England; having that force of thought and that sense of right which are the warp and woof of greatness. Our farmers were Orthodox Calvinists, mighty in the Scriptures; had learned that life was a preparation, a "probation," to use their word, for a higher world, and was to be spent in loving and serving mankind.

Thus was formed a romantic character absolutely without any vulgar trait; living to ideal ends, without any mixture of self-indulgence or compromise, such as lowers the value of benevolent and thoughtful men we know; abstemious, refusing luxuries, not sourly and reproachfully, but simply as unfit for his habit; quiet and gentle as a child in the house. And, as happens usually to men of romantic character, his fortunes were romantic. Walter Scott would have delighted to draw his picture and trace his adventurous career. A shepherd and herdsman, he learned the manners of animals, and knew the secret signals by which animals communicate. He made his hard bed on the mountains with them; he learned to drive his flock through thickets all but impassable; he had all the skill of a shepherd by choice of breed and by wise husbandry to obtain the best wool, and that for a course of years. And the anecdotes preserved show a far-seeing skill and conduct which, in spite of adverse accidents, should secure, one year with another, an honest reward, first to the farmer, and afterwards to the dealer. If he kept sheep, it was with a royal mind; and if he traded in wool, he was a merchant prince, not in the amount of wealth, but in the protection of the interests confided to him.

I am not a little surprised at the easy effrontery with which political gentlemen, in and out of Congress, take it upon them to say that there are not a thousand men in the North who sympathize with John Brown. It would be far safer and nearer the truth to say that all people, in proportion to their sensibility and self-respect, sympathize with him. For it is impossible to see courage, and disinterestedness, and the love that casts out fear, without sympathy. All women are drawn to him by their predominance of sentiment. All gentlemen, of course, are on his side. I do not mean by "gentlemen," people of scented hair and perfumed handkerchiefs, but men of gentle blood and generosity, "fulfilled with all nobleness," who, like the Cid, give the outcast leper a share of their bed; like the dying Sidney, pass the cup of cold water to the dying soldier who needs it more. For what is the oath of gentle blood and knighthood? What but to protect the weak and lowly against the strong oppressor?

Nothing is more absurd than to complain of this sympathy, or to complain of a party of men united in opposition to slavery. As well complain of gravity, or the ebb of the tide. Who makes the abolitionist? The slave-holder. The sentiment of mercy is the natural recoil which the laws of the universe provide to protect man-kind from destruction by savage passions. And our blind statesmen go up and down, with committees of vigilance and safety, hunting for the origin of this new heresy. They will need a very vigilant committee indeed to find its birthplace, and a very strong force to root it out. For the arch-abolitionist, older than Brown, and older than the Shenandoah Mountains, is Love, whose other name is Justice, which was before Alfred, before Lycurgus, before slavery, and will be after it.

THOREAU, THE LAST DAYS OF JOHN BROWN (1860)

Emerson's influence, his John Brown lectures, and Thoreau's "Plea for Captain John Brown" provide context for "The Last Days of John Brown," a speech given nine months after "Plea." In many ways, the focus of "Plea" is the calling out of newspaper editors, in the same way that Martin Luther King, Jr. called out moderate clergy in "Letter from Birmingham Jail." In King's case, the clergy didn't understand the necessity of nonviolent activism and taking it to the streets; in Brown's case, the newspaper editors didn't understand his turn to violence in response to violence. But what the newspaper editors mostly didn't get is John Brown himself. And so, Thoreau spoke out and spelt it out.

Newspaper editors wondered what Brown gained at Harpers Ferry, seeing no point in the risky attack. Thoreau responded that the editors think in terms of material things when they should think in terms of soul, which then has material effects. But, since they lack the vitality of soul, which is the ultimate vice, that "stagnation of spirit" makes them unable to understand Brown's motives. They consider their feeble response to slavery as sane, and so Brown's robust actions must be insane. Thoreau argued they would have to "enlarge themselves" to judge him, but, since they are incapable of doing so, he has no peers.

Thoreau further argued that the editors, since they are out of touch with soul, cannot print the truth. Brown did not seek revenge, as many claimed, but acted on behalf of the oppressed. They should listen to Brown's own words before he was hanged: "I pity the poor in bondage that have none to help them; that is why I am here, not to gratify any personal animosity, revenge, or vindictive spirit. It is my sympathy with the oppressed and the wronged, that are as good as you, and as precious in the sight of God."

Thoreau knew that the "monster of government," not the newspaper editors, was most at fault, as the government was not representing the people because they were not representing their human potential. In "Plea" and "Last Days," Thoreau flipped the narrative, forcing citizens, and the editors, to question who is virtuous and who is not. He called Brown "the most American of us all," making hearers and readers identify with Brown, or to sympathize with him and make radical action seem necessary rather than extreme.

Thoreau, in "Plea," pleads for his legacy, for his immortal life more than his life, which is a lost cause. He continues this theme in "The Last Days of John Brown." Brown did not fear death, and by teaching us how to die, he teaches us how to live; his critics know nothing about "living and dying for a principle." Fear is a restraint, and so overcoming fear removes a barrier to action. That's another high bar, but Thoreau wants to turn Brown's death into a new beginning.

That beginning is articulated in "Last Days," where he states: "The man this country was about to hang appeared the greatest and best in it." Like Emerson, Thoreau knew that Brown was more Calvinist than transcendentalist, as he saw himself as an instrument of God. That claim most certainly has its dangers. History is littered with so-called "holy" wars bolstered by self-deception. Still, Thoreau saw the transcendentalist in him, and the Christ in him, and brought it out for all to ponder, learn from, and ultimately embody in our actions. Brown defended liberty for all, not just the wealthy white male few, and we should do the same.

Yet, can we all be John Browns? Should we want to be? Isn't that asking too much? At the least, he provokes us to ask questions of conscience. Thoreau's defense of Brown is clearly linked to his call to follow conscience in "Civil Disobedience." What Thoreau argued for in his seminal essay, Brown lived. Thoreau wants us to overcome reticence and embrace resistance. Again, there are many ways to make a contribution, and violence, depending on how it is defined and practiced, may not be the way, or may never be the way. But some are following the more radical path of Brown.

In the summer of 2017, Ruby Montoya and Jessica Reznicek admitted to numerous acts of arson and property damage to the Dakota Access pipeline, which ignored Sioux sovereignty, threatened water supply and soil with oil contamination, and increased fossil fuel infrastructure that undermines planetary well-being. They knew they would be sent to jail, and willingly went to draw attention to their cause. Their statement included the following: "Some may view these actions as violent, but be not mistaken. We acted from our hearts and never threatened human life nor personal property... What we did do was fight a private corporation that has run rampant across our country, seizing land and polluting our nation's water supply. You may not agree with our tactics, but you can clearly see their necessity in light of the broken federal government and the corporations they represent."

To the FBI, Montoya and Reznicek are domestic eco-terrorists, but the echoes of John Brown live on, as well as Thoreau's stirring defense of him. In "Last Days" he seizes the moral moment, but also the narrative moment. Thoreau uses words as weapons to argue for a post-Brown world of active souls.

SOURCES

Shipley, Julia. "You Strike a Match: Why Two Women Risked Everything to Stop the Dakota Access Pipeline." Grist.org. May 26, 2021.

Turner, Jack. "Thoreau and John Brown. In *The Political Companion to Henry David Thoreau*. Edited by Jack Turner. Lexington: The University Press of Kentucky, 2009.

Walls, Laura Dassow. *Henry David Thoreau: A Life*. Chicago: The University of Chicago Press, 2017.

THE LAST DAYS OF JOHN BROWN

Henry David Thoreau

John Brown's career for the last six weeks of his life was meteor-like, flashing through the darkness in which we live. I know of nothing so miraculous in our history.

If any person, in a lecture or conversation at that time, cited any ancient example of heroism, such as Cato or Tell or Winkelried, passing over the recent deeds and words of Brown, it was felt by any intelligent audience of Northern men to be tame and inexcusably far-fetched.

For my own part, I commonly attend more to nature than to man, but any affecting human event may blind our eyes to natural objects. I was so absorbed in him as to be surprised whenever I detected the routine of the natural world surviving still, or met persons going about their affairs indifferent. It appeared strange to me that the "little dipper" should be still diving quietly into the river, as of yore; and it suggested that this bird might continue to dive here when Concord should be no more.

I felt that he, a prisoner in the midst of his enemies and under sentence of death, if consulted as to his next step or resource, could answer more wisely than all his countrymen beside. He best understood his position; he contemplated it most calmly. Comparatively, all other men, North and South, were beside themselves. Our thoughts could not revert to any greater or wiser or better man with whom to contrast him, for he, then and there, was above them all. The man this country was about to hang appeared the greatest and best in it.

Years were not required for a revolution of public opinion; days, nay hours, produced marked changes in this case. Fifty who were ready to say, on going into our meeting in honor of him in Concord, that he ought to be hung, would not say it when they came out. They heard his words read; they saw the earnest faces of the congregation; and perhaps they joined at last in singing the hymn in his praise.

The order of instructions was reversed. I heard that one preacher, who at first was shocked and stood aloof, felt obliged at last, after he was hung, to make him the subject of a sermon, in which, to some extent, he eulogized the man, but said that his act was a failure. An influential class-teacher thought it necessary, after the services, to tell his grown-up pupils that at first he thought as the preacher did then, but now he thought that John Brown was right. But it was understood that his pupils were as much ahead of the teacher as he was ahead of the priest; and I know for a certainty that very little boys at home had already asked their parents, in a tone of surprise, why God did not interfere to save him. In each case, the constituted teachers were only half conscious that they were not leading, but being dragged, with some loss of time and power.

The more conscientious preachers, the Bible men, they who talk about principle, and doing to others as you would that they should do unto you,—how could they fail to recognize him, by far the greatest preacher of them all, with the Bible in his life and in his acts, the embodiment of principle, who actually carried out the golden rule? All whose moral sense had been aroused, who had a calling from on high to preach, sided with him. What confessions he extracted from the cold and conservative! It is remarkable, but on the whole it is well, that it did not prove the occasion for a new sect of Brownites being formed in our midst.

They, whether within the Church or out of it, who adhere to the spirit and let go the letter, and are accordingly called infidel, were as usual foremost to recognize him. Men have been hung in the South before for attempting to rescue slaves, and the North was not much stirred by it. Whence, then, this wonderful difference? We were not so sure of their devotion to principle. We made a subtle distinction, forgot human laws, and did homage to an idea. The North, I mean the living North, was suddenly all transcendental. It went behind the human law, it went behind the apparent failure, and recognized eternal justice and glory. Commonly, men live according to a formula, and are satisfied if the order of law is observed, but in this instance they, to some extent, returned to original perceptions, and there was a slight revival of old religion. They saw that what was called order was confusion, what was called justice, injustice, and that the best was deemed the worst. This attitude suggested a more intelligent and generous spirit than that which actuated our forefathers, and the possibility, in the course of ages, of a revolution in behalf of another and an oppressed people.

Most Northern men, and a few Southern ones, were wonderfully stirred by Brown's behavior and words. They saw and felt that they were heroic and noble, and that there had been nothing quite equal to them in their kind in this country, or in the recent history of the world. But the minority were unmoved by them. They were only surprised and provoked by the attitude of their neighbors. They saw that

Brown was brave, and that he believed that he had done right, but they did not detect any further peculiarity in him. Not being accustomed to make fine distinctions, or to appreciate magnanimity, they read his letters and speeches as if they read them not. They were not aware when they approached a heroic statement,—they did not know when they burned. They did not feel that he spoke with authority, and hence they only remembered that the law must be executed. They remembered the old formula, but did not hear the new revelation. The man who does not recognize in Brown's words a wisdom and nobleness, and therefore an authority, superior to our laws, is a modern Democrat. This is the test by which to discover him. He is not willfully but constitutionally blind on this side, and he is consistent with himself. Such has been his past life; no doubt of it. In like manner he has read history and his Bible, and he accepts, or seems to accept, the last only as an established formula, and not because he has been convicted by it. You will not find kindred sentiments in his commonplace-book, if he has one.

When a noble deed is done, who is likely to appreciate it? They who are noble themselves. I was not surprised that certain of my neighbors spoke of John Brown as an ordinary felon, for who are they? They have either much flesh, or much office, or much coarseness of some kind. They are not ethereal natures in any sense. The dark qualities predominate in them. Several of them are decidedly pachydermatous. I say it in sorrow, not in anger. How can a man behold the light who has no answering inward light? They are true to their sight, but when they look this way they see nothing, they are blind. For the children of the light to contend with them is as if there should be a contest between eagles and owls. Show me a man who feels bitterly toward John Brown, and let me hear what noble verse he can repeat. He'll be as dumb as if his lips were stone.

It is not every man who can be a Christian, even in a very moderate sense, whatever education you give him. It is a matter of constitution and temperament, after all. He may have to be born again many times. I have known many a man who pretended to be a Christian, in whom it was ridiculous, for he had no genius for it. It is not every man who can be a free man, even.

Editors persevered for a good while in saying that Brown was crazy; but at last they said only that it was "a crazy scheme," and the only evidence brought to prove it was that it cost him his life. I have no doubt that if he had gone with five thousand men, liberated a thousand slaves, killed a hundred or two slaveholders, and had as many more killed on his own side, but not lost his own life, these same editors would have called it by a more respectable name. Yet he has been far more successful than that. He has liberated many thousands of slaves, both North and South. They seem to have known nothing about living or dying for a principle. They all called him crazy then; who calls him crazy now?

All through the excitement occasioned by his remarkable attempt and subsequent behavior the Massachusetts legislature, not taking any steps for the defense of her citizens who were likely to be carried to Virginia as witnesses and exposed to the violence of a slaveholding mob, was wholly absorbed in a liquor-agency question, and indulging in poor jokes on the word "extension." Bad spirits occupied their thoughts. I am sure that no statesman up to the occasion could have attended to that question at all at that time, — a very vulgar question to attend to at any time!

When I looked into a liturgy of the Church of England, printed near the end of the last century, in order to find a service applicable to the case of Brown, I found that the only martyr recognized and provided for it was King Charles the First, an eminent scamp. Of all the inhabitants of England and of the world, he was the only one, according to this authority, whom that church had made a martyr and saint of; and for more than a century it had celebrated his martyrdom, so called, by an annual service. What a satire on the Church is that!

Look not to legislatures and churches for your guidance, nor to any soulless incorporated bodies, but to inspirited or inspired ones.

What avail all your scholarly accomplishments and learning, compared with wisdom and manhood? To omit his other behavior, see what a work this comparatively unread and unlettered man wrote within six weeks. Where is our professor of belles-lettres, or of logic and rhetoric, who can write so well? He wrote in prison, not a History of the World, like Raleigh, but an American book which I think will live longer than that. I do not know of such words, uttered under such circumstances, and so copiously withal, in Roman or English or any history. What a variety of themes he touched on in that short space! There are words in that letter to his wife, respecting the education of his daughters, which deserve to be framed and hung over every mantelpiece in the land. Compare this earnest wisdom with that of Poor Richard.

Thoreau, "The Last Days of John Brown" (1860)

The death of Irving, which at any other time would have attracted universal attention, having occurred while these things were transpiring, went almost unobserved. I shall have to read of it in the biography of authors.

Literary gentlemen, editors, and critics think that they know how to write, because they have studied grammar and rhetoric; but they are egregiously mistaken. The art of composition is as simple as the discharge of a bullet from a rifle, and its masterpieces imply an infinitely greater force behind them. This unlettered man's speaking and writing are standard English. Some words and phrases deemed vulgarisms and Americanisms before, he has made standard American; such as "It will pay." It suggests that the one great rule of composition—and if I were a professor of rhetoric I should insist on this—is, to speak the truth. This first, this second, this third; pebbles in your mouth or not. This demands earnestness and manhood chiefly.

We seem to have forgotten that the expression "a liberal education" originally meant among the Romans one worthy of free men; while the learning of trades and professions by which to get your livelihood merely was considered worthy of slaves only. But taking a hint from the word, I would go a step further, and say that it is not the man of wealth and leisure simply, though devoted to art, or science, or literature, who, in a true sense, is liberally educated, but only the earnest and free man. In a slaveholding country like this, there can be no such thing as a liberal education tolerated by the State; and those scholars of Austria and France who, however learned they may be, are contented under their tyrannies have received only a servile education.

Nothing could his enemies do but it redounded to his infinite advantage,—that is, to the advantage of his cause. They did not hang him at once, but reserved him to preach to them. And then there was another great blunder. They did not hang his four followers with him; that scene was still postponed; and so his victory was prolonged and completed. No theatrical manager could have arranged things so wisely to give effect to his behavior and words. And who, think you, was the manager? Who placed the slave-woman and her child, whom he stooped to kiss for a symbol, between his prison and the gallows?

We soon saw, as he saw, that he was not to be pardoned or rescued by men. That would have been to disarm him, to restore him a material weapon, a Sharp's rifle, when he had taken up the sword of the spirit,—the sword with which he has really won his greatest and most memorable victories. Now he has not laid aside the sword of the spirit, for he is pure spirit himself, and his sword is pure spirit also.

> "He nothing common did or mean
> Upon that memorable scene, ...
> Nor called the gods with vulgar spite,
> To vindicate his helpless right;
> But bowed his comely head
> Down, as upon a bed."

What a transit was that of his horizontal body alone, but just cut down from the gallows-tree! We read that at such a time it passed through Philadelphia, and by Saturday night had reached New York. Thus like a meteor it shot through the Union from the Southern regions toward the North! No such freight had the cars borne since they carried him southward alive.

On the day of his translation, I heard, to be sure, that he was hung, but I did not know what that meant; I felt no sorrow on that account; but not for a day or two did I even hear that he was dead, and not after any number of days shall I believe it. Of all the men who were said to be my contemporaries, it seemed to me that John Brown was the only one who had not died. I never hear of a man named Brown now,—and I hear of them pretty often,—I never hear of any particularly brave and earnest man, but my first thought is of John Brown, and what relation he may be to him. I meet him at every turn. He is more alive than he ever was. He has earned immortality. He is not confined to North Elba nor to Kansas. He is no longer working in secret. He works in public, and in the clearest light that shines on this land.

WORKS CITED

Andrews, Barry. *Transcendentalism and the Cultivation of the Soul*. Amherst: The University of Massachusetts Press, 2017.

———. *American Sage: The Spiritual Teachings of Ralph Waldo Emerson*. Amherst: The University of Massachusetts Press, 2021.

Balthrop-Lewis, Alda. *Thoreau's Religion: Walden Woods, Social Justice, and the Politics of Asceticism*. Cambridge: Cambridge University Press, 2021.

Boyd, Andrew. *I Want a Better Catastrophe: Navigating the Climate Crisis with Grief, Hope, and Gallows Humor*. British Columbia: New Society Publishers, 2023.

Buber, Martin. *I and Thou*. Translated and edited by Walter Kaufmann. New York: Scribner's, 1970.

Buehrens, John A. Conflagration: *How the Transcendentalists Sparked the American Struggle for Racial, Gender, and Social Justice*. Boston: Beacon Press Books, 2020.

Buell, Lawrence. *Emerson*. Cambridge: Harvard University Press, 2003.

———. *Henry David Thoreau: Thinking Disobediently*. Oxford: Oxford University Press, 2023.

Buell, Lawrence, editor. *The American Transcendentalists: Essential Writings*. New York: Modern Library, 2006.

Chenoweth, Erica. *Civil Resistance: What Everyone Needs to Know*. London: Oxford University Press, 2021.

Emerson, Ralph Waldo. *The Portable Emerson*. Edited by Carl Bode & Malcolm Cowley. New York: Penguin Books, 1981.

———. *The Political Emerson*. Edited by David M. Robinson. Boston: Beacon Press, 2004.

———. *Emerson's Antislavery Writings*. Edited by Len Gougeon and Joel Myerson. New Haven: Yale University Press, 1995.

———. *The Essential Writings of Ralph Waldo Emerson*. New York: Random House Modern Library Classics, 2000.

Emerson, R. W., & Thoreau, H. D. *Nature/Walking*. Edited by John Elder. Boston: Beacon Press, 1991.

Harding, Walter. *The Days of Henry Thoreau: A Biography*. Princeton: Princeton University Press, 1962.

Hawken, Paul. *Blessed Unrest: How the Largest Social Movement in History is Restoring Grace, Justice, and Beauty to the World*. New York: Penguin Books, 2008.

———. *Regeneration: Ending the Climate Crisis in One Generation*. New York: Penguin Books, 2021.

Hopkins, Hop. "Racism is Killing the Planet," *Sierra: The Magazine of the Sierra Club*, June 8, 2020.

Kucich, John J. "Thoreau's Indian Problem: Savagism, Indigeneity, and the Politics of Place." In *Thoreau in an Age of Crisis: Uses and Abuses of an American Icon*. Edited by Kriste Case, Rochelle Johnson, and Henrik Otterberg. Paderborn, Germany: Brill-Fink, 2021.

Levine, Alan M. and Daniel S. Malachuk, editors. *A Political Companion to Ralph Waldo Emerson*. Lexington: The University Press of Kentucky, 2011.

Malm, Andreas. *How to Blow Up a Pipeline*. New York: Verso Books, 2021.

Marcus, James. *Glad to the Brink of Fear: A Portrait of Ralph Waldo Emerson*. Princeton: Princeton University Press, 2024.

Works Cited

Marshall, Megan. *Margaret Fuller: A New American Life*. New York: Mariner Books, 2013.

Painter, Nell Irvin. *The History of White People*. New York: W. W. Norton and Co., 2010.

PBS. "John Brown's Holy War: Pottawatomie Massacre," *The American Experience*, February 28, 2000.

Petrulionis, Sandra Harbert. "Between 'That Farthest Western Way' and 'The University of the West.'" In *Thoreau Beyond Borders: New International Essays on America's Most Famous Nature Writer*. Edited by Francois Specq, Laura Dassow Walls, and Julien Negre. Amherst: University of Massachusetts Press, 2020.

Reynold, David S. "Transcendentalism, Transnationalism, and Antislavery Violence: Concord's Embrace of John Brown." In *Emerson for the 21st Century*. Edited by Barry Tharaud. Delaware: University of Delaware Press, 2010.

Richardson, Richard D. Jr.'s *Emerson: The Mind on Fire*. Berkeley, CA: University of California Press, 1995.

Schmitz, Michael. "Trump Embraces Lawlessness, but in the Name of a Higher Law." *The New York Times*, May 2, 2024.

Shipley, Julia. "You Strike a Match: Why Two Women Risked Everything to Stop the Dakota Access Pipeline." Grist.org. May 26, 2021.

Stephenson, Wen. *What We're Fighting for Now is Each Other: Dispatches from the Front Lines of Climate Justice*. Boston: Beacon Press, 2015.

Thoreau, Henry David. *The Portable Thoreau*. Edited by Carl Bode. New York: Penguin Books, 1975.

———. *Civil Disobedience*. Edited by Bob Pepperman Taylor. Ontario, Canada: Broadview Press, 2016.

Turner, Jack, editor. "Introduction." In *The Political Companion to Henry David Thoreau*. Lexington: The University of Kentucky Press. 2009.

Turner, Jack. "Thoreau and John Brown. In *The Political Companion to Henry David Thoreau*. Edited by Jack Turner. Lexington: The University Press of Kentucky, 2009.

Walls, Laura Dassow. *Henry David Thoreau: A Life*. Chicago: The University of Chicago Press, 2017.

———. "Counter Frictions: Thoreau and the Integral Commons." In *Thoreau Beyond Borders: International Essays on America's Most Famous Nature Writer*. Edited by Francois Specq, Laura Dassow Walls, and Julien Negre. Amherst: University of Massachusetts Press, 2020.

Waxman, Olivia B. "What to the Slave is the Fourth of July? The History of Frederick Douglass' Searing Independence Day Oration." *Time Magazine*. June 26, 2020. Time.com.

Wirzbicki, Peter. *Fighting for the Higher Law: Black and White Transcendentalists Against Slavery*. Philadelphia: University of Pennsylvania Press, 2021.